Bear Grylls

EPIC FLIGHTS

Discover more amazing books in the Bear Grylls series:

Perfect for young adventurers, the *Epic Adventures* series accompanies an exciting range of colouring and activity books, and a fantastic series of *Survival Skills* handbooks to help them explore the wild. Curious kids can also explore Earth in *Extreme Planet*, and learn tips and tricks for almost any extreme situation in *Survival Camp*.

Conceived by Weldon Owen in partnership with Bear Grylls Ventures

Produced by Weldon Owen, an imprint of Kings Road Publishing
Suite 3.08 The Plaza, 535 Kings Road,
London SW10 0SZ, UK

WELDON OWEN
Editor Susie Rae
Designer Shahid Mahmood
Text by Von Hardesty
Contributor Andy Briggs
Cover photograph copyright © Getty Images

Printed in Malaysia
2 4 6 8 10 9 7 5 3 1

Disclaimer
Weldon Owen and Bear Grylls take pride in doing our best to get the facts right in putting together the information in this book, but occasionally something slips past our beady eyes. Therefore we make no warranties about the accuracy or completeness of the information in the book, and to the maximum extent permitted, we disclaim all liability. Wherever possible, we will endeavour to correct any errors of fact at reprint.

Kids – if you want to try any of the activities in this book, please ask your parents first! Parents – all outdoor activities carry some degree of risk and we recommend that anyone participating in these activities be aware of the risks involved and seek professional instruction and guidance. None of the health/medical information in this book is intended as a substitute for professional medical advice; always seek the advice of a qualified practitioner.

A WELDON OWEN PRODUCTION. AN IMPRINT OF KINGS ROAD PUBLISHING.
PART OF THE BONNIER PUBLISHING GROUP.

EPIC
FLIGHTS

CONTENTS

 # Bear Grylls

Epic Flights

Human beings have been exploring the land and sea for centuries, discovering all that our planet has to offer, but it has only been in the past century or so that we have been able to begin exploring the skies. Since the Wright brothers first invented the aeroplane, people have raced to set record after record – who can fly the fastest, the furthest, and for the longest? Only 66 years after the first ever flight, humanity achieved something that had previously been thought impossible, when Neil Armstrong and Buzz Aldrin set foot on the Moon, showing the true spirit of adventure that makes humanity so amazing.

Aviation has opened up so many new and exciting ways to travel and places to explore.

I've been lucky enough to work with some amazing aviators in my time, from the SAS to stunt pilots and everything in between. People like this are an endless source of inspiration to me.

Facing your fears

Since I fractured my spine after a parachuting accident many years ago, I have been terrified of parachute jumping – but that hasn't stopped me! Even though it can be hard, it's important to get out there and face up to your fears. After all, if all of the incredible aviators and explorers in this book had avoided doing things that scared them, they would never have got off the ground!

Spirit of St. Louis

Charles Lindbergh

Excitement in the Air

Early in the 20th century, aviation emerged as one of the most competitive spheres of human activity. Bold men and women vied with one another to fly "faster, further, and higher". Barnstormers, or stunt pilots, thrilled throngs of aviation enthusiasts at air shows. The aeroplane itself underwent a radical transformation, with sleek monoplanes replacing the slow and cumbersome biplanes of old. The Wright Whirlwind radial engine offered the safety and reliability essential for long-distance flying. Visionaries imagined a more closely linked world, with aeroplanes carrying people across vast distances. Uncharted realms could now be explored. The air age became an arena for individual heroism.

Charles Lindbergh stands in front of his iconic biplane, *Spirit of St. Louis.*

The *Spirit of St. Louis* flies through the air on her history-making flight.

Four landmark flights prior to the crossing of the Atlantic

1903
American brothers Orville and Wilbur Wright made the world's first powered flight in the *Wright Flyer*, travelling only 37 m.

1909
Frenchman Louis Blériot, in a fragile and unreliable monoplane, made the first flight across the English Channel, winning a £1,000 prize offered by London's *Daily Mail*.

1911
American pioneer aviator Calbraith "Cal" Rodgers made the first transcontinental flight across the United States, in a biplane with no instruments.

1914
Russian aircraft designer Igor Sikorsky flew his four-engine *Il'ya Muromets* from St. Petersburg to Kiev and back, covering a distance of 1,280 km.

BEAR SAYS

Early aviation wasn't all successes – in May 1927, Charles Nungesser and François Coli disappeared without a trace in their biplane *L'Oiseau Blanc* ("white bird") while attempting to cross the Atlantic Ocean.

Richard Byrd

US naval officer Richard Byrd (right) claimed to be the first person to reach both the North and South Poles by air in 1926 and 1929, though this claim has been disputed.

The race to cross the Atlantic

In 1919, New York hotelier Raymond Orteig offered a $25,000 prize to the first aviator to fly nonstop from New York to Paris. By 1927, the competition was intense. Richard Byrd and Clarence Chamberlin were the favourites. An unknown young contender named Charles Lindbergh planned to fly solo.

Ill-fated attempt

In his attempt to win the Orteig Prize in 1926, celebrated French ace René Fonck (below) crashed on takeoff in his Sikorsky-designed S-35 trimotor.

BEAR SAYS

Early aircraft didn't have the power to lift the amount of fuel needed to cross the Atlantic – this was a major challenge for anyone competing for the Orteig Prize.

The wreckage of Alcock and Brown's plane after their successful transatlantic flight.

First across the North Atlantic

In 1919, British aviators John Alcock and Arthur Brown (right) flew a World War I Vickers Vimy bomber nonstop across the North Atlantic, from Newfoundland to Ireland. Their 3,040-km flight through fog, snow, and ice took 15 hours and 57 minutes. They won a £10,000 *Daily Mail* prize and were knighted by King George V.

Inglorious end

Alcock and Brown crash-landed in an Irish bog near Clifden, plowing into the mud. They emerged unscathed.

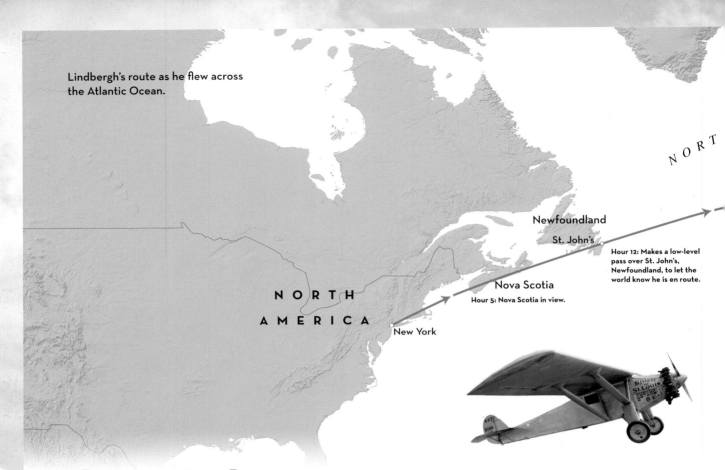

Lindbergh's route as he flew across the Atlantic Ocean.

NORTH AMERICA

Newfoundland
St. John's

Nova Scotia

Hour 5: Nova Scotia in view.

Hour 12: Makes a low-level pass over St. John's, Newfoundland, to let the world know he is en route.

New York

N O R T

Flying Solo

He was young and unknown, the press ignored him, and many called him a "flying fool" for his bold plan to fly solo across the Atlantic. Charles Lindbergh came to the transatlantic competition with many hours of high-risk flying under his belt, as a barnstormer, a mail pilot, and a veteran of the US Army Air Service. He designed his *Spirit of St. Louis* to remain airborne for 40 hours, if necessary. His flight plan was carefully laid out. To save weight, he took minimal survival equipment. Most importantly, he had a powerful desire to achieve his goal. While his rivals dallied, Lindbergh seized his chance. He took off from Roosevelt Field, Long Island, at 7:52 am on 20th May 1927.

ATLANTIC OCEAN

Hour 28: Irish coast appears on the horizon. Sights Cape Valentia and Dingle Bay.

Ireland

London

Dingle Bay

Hour 22: Falls asleep repeatedly over the storm-tossed Atlantic, but maintains course.

Cherbourg

Paris

Hour 33: Lands at Le Bourget airport.

Hour 32: Flies over Cherbourg, on the French coast.

EUROPE

AFRICA

Travelling light

The few personal items Lindbergh took with him included a passport, a canteen, and a torch. He later expressed concern over arriving in Paris without a visa or diplomatic clearance.

BEAR SAYS

Always facing up to danger, Lindbergh survived four crashes before his legendary Atlantic flight, bailing out and parachuting to safety.

Weighing up the odds

On his transatlantic flight, determined to keep weight to a minimum, Charles Lindbergh carried a rubber raft in case of a water landing, but did not take a parachute.

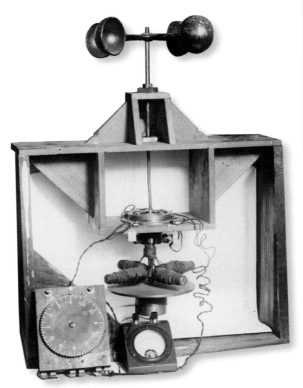

Finding his way

For navigation, Charles Lindbergh chose an Earth Inductor Compass, which allowed him to correct for Earth's magnetic deviation, and a standard magnetic compass.

Jolted awake

Lindbergh designed his fabled *Spirit of St. Louis* to be an "unstable" plane – to ensure he would stay awake for the entire journey across the Atlantic.

Race rivals

In May 1927, underdog Charles Lindbergh greeted the race favourites, Richard Byrd and Clarence Chamberlin (left). While his rivals delayed, Lindbergh boldly set out in the *Spirit of St. Louis*, a brave risk that would ultimately win him the race across the Atlantic.

First landfall

Some 28 hours into the flight, with a perilous night crossing of the North Atlantic behind him, Lindbergh sighted the Irish coast. Now Paris beckoned, just five hours away.

BEAR SAYS

Between pre-flight preparations and the 33.5-hour flight, Lindbergh was awake for 55 hours. At times, he skimmed the surface of the sea to wake himself up with the cold spray.

Charles Lindbergh's transatlantic flight was the crowning achievement in a line of pioneering aviation feats that started with the Wright brothers' flight at Kitty Hawk in 1903.

Destination: Paris

For those of us who routinely fly across continents and oceans today, it is difficult to fully comprehend the dangers Charles Lindbergh faced on his transatlantic flight. He followed the "great circle" route, the shortest distance between two points on a sphere. The arc of this flight path carried him over Nova Scotia and Newfoundland, across 3,200 km of open ocean, to the coasts of Ireland and England, to Cherbourg, and finally to Paris, where he landed at Le Bourget airport at 10:22 pm on 21st May 1927 – after a flight lasting 33 hours, 30 minutes, and 29.8 seconds. He had flown through fog, rain, and headwinds. The *Spirit of St. Louis* had performed flawlessly. His biggest challenge had been staying awake.

All mapped out

Charles Lindbergh used a "Time Zone Chart of the World" to lay out his route from New York to Paris. The flight was sketched out in segments along the "great circle" route.

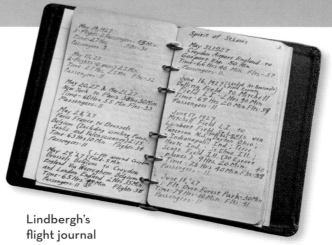

Lindbergh's flight journal

The "great circle" route

Charles Lindbergh cleverly calculated the shortest route from New York to Paris. Because of the way the Earth curves, the shortest distance between two points on the globe is on the arc of a circle that would divide the Earth into two equal parts and that passes through those points. This is called a great circle. (You can test this by stretching a piece of string around a globe). This route required Lindbergh to change course every 160 km, around once an hour.

Souvenir hunters

The *Spirit of St. Louis* lands triumphantly in Paris (right) after Lindbergh's historic flight. The plane had to be repaired when jubilant crowds tore off pieces of fabric for souvenirs.

Skill and Courage

At the controls of an airplane, he fascinated the world. Flying from New York to Paris in his beloved *Spirit of St. Louis* won him instant fame. Many saw in Lindbergh the ideal of heroism. His stunning feat of flying the Atlantic solo was just one episode in a larger career of risk-taking. As a barnstormer in the early 1920s, he had performed many death-defying aerobatic feats, to the delight of enthusiastic crowds. Flying the airmail routes, often in bad weather or at night, he displayed his impressive skills as a pilot. He survived many crashes, including a mid-air collision while in the US Army Air Service. What many did not see behind this image of bold aviator were Lindbergh's engineering skills and his belief that the aeroplane would soon transform modern life.

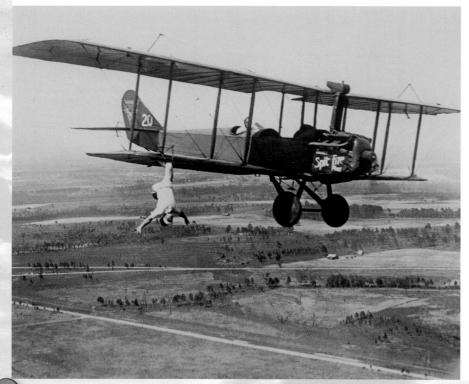

Barnstorming

Charles Lindbergh loved speed and risk-taking. As a newly licensed pilot, he decided to enter the world of the "barnstormers", or stunt pilots. These touring aviators routinely, and for modest wages, performed "death-defying" aerobatic feats such as loops, rolls, stalls, and wing-walking. "Daredevil Lindbergh", as he became known, thrived in this dangerous profession.

Rain or shine

Airmail pilots had to maintain precise schedules and fly in all kinds of weather. Night flying in open-cockpit planes, often without good navigation aids, could spell disaster.

Army service

After his stunt days, Lindbergh joined the US Army Air Service, winning his wings at Kelly Field in Texas. He flew with the 110th Observation Squadron of the Missouri National Guard.

Quietly confident

On his flight, Charles Lindbergh carried a letter addressed to James F. Prince of the Wright Aeronautical Corporation confirming his arrival in Paris. He planned to post it, but instead it was sent by diplomatic pouch.

In this photograph, taken in 1909, the young Charles stands beside his father, Charles August Lindbergh. His father was an independent congressman from the US state of Minnesota.

Spirit of St. Louis statistics	
Length	8 m
Height	3 m
Wingspan	14 m
Gross weight	2,330 kg
Engine	Wright Whirlwind J-5C, 223 hp (166 kW)

Spirit of St. Louis

The *Spirit of St. Louis* was designed for one purpose – to conquer the Atlantic. It was a sleek monoplane, its modern streamlining evident in its cowling, wings, and landing gear. Huge fuel tanks were fitted to the fuselage and wings. The emphasis was on sturdy, lightweight materials. The fuselage was framed in tubular steel. The wings and ribs, covered in a thin cotton fabric coated with aluminium-hue dope, were built with the best spruce and mahogany wood components. A single Wright Whirlwind engine powered this special long-distance aircraft. Since the main fuel tanks were mounted ahead of the cockpit, Lindbergh could not see directly ahead, except by using a periscope on the left side, or banking and looking out the side window.

Cabin in the sky

Lindbergh referred to his cockpit as his "cabin in the sky". The tiny cockpit was so cramped that Lindbergh couldn't stretch his legs for the whole flight. His compass was mounted on the wall behind him, and he read it using a pocket mirror which he stuck to the ceiling using chewing gum.

Memorabilia

In later years, Lindbergh placed flag decals of many nations on the nose cowling of the *Spirit of St. Louis* as a record of his many flights. By the time the aircraft was retired, it had made a total of 174 flights.

Wicker seat

To save weight, Lindbergh chose a wicker seat. The built-in discomfort was an advantage – it helped to keep him awake during the long flight.

Wright Whirlwind radial engine

Charles Lindbergh chose the 223 hp (166 kW) J-5C version of the durable Wright Whirlwind radial engine for the *Spirit of St. Louis*. The Wright Whirlwind made long-distance flying safe. At that time, it had the world's most advanced aero propulsion system. It also had an excellent power-to-weight ratio, guaranteeing maximum lift for the *Spirit of St. Louis* when it took off with full fuel tanks.

State of the art

The *Spirit of St. Louis* was a monoplane with many streamlined contours. The several fuel tanks were cleverly integrated into the fuselage and wings.

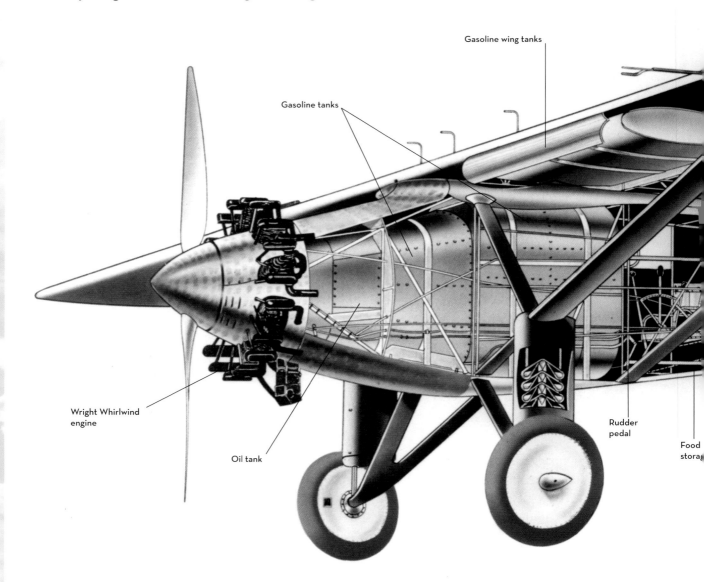

Gasoline wing tanks

Gasoline tanks

Wright Whirlwind engine

Oil tank

Rudder pedal

Food storage

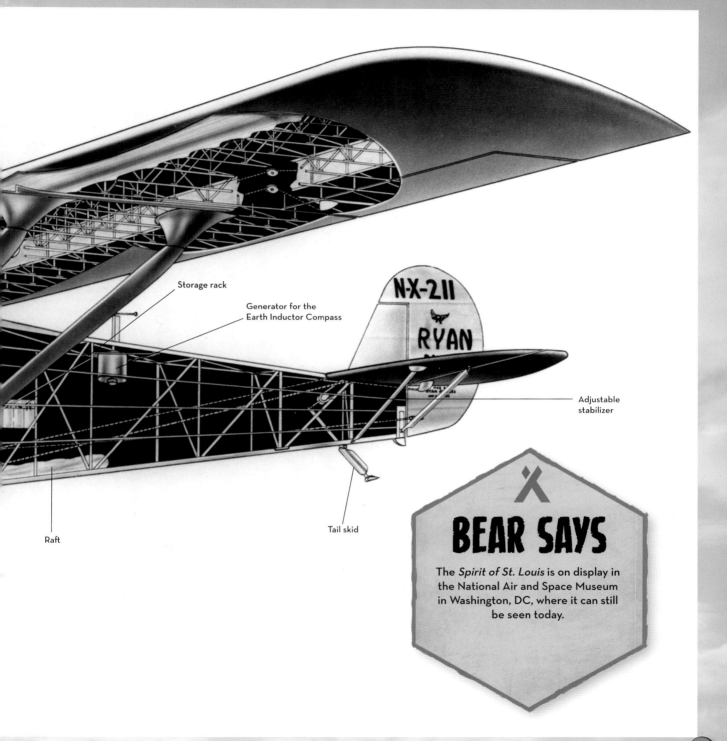

Storage rack

Generator for the
Earth Inductor Compass

N·X-211
RYAN

Adjustable
stabilizer

Tail skid

Raft

BEAR SAYS

The *Spirit of St. Louis* is on display in
the National Air and Space Museum
in Washington, DC, where it can still
be seen today.

All Hail the Hero!

People around the world reacted to Charles Lindbergh's transatlantic flight with awe and jubilation. As Lindbergh himself said, the effect was "like a match lighting a bonfire". A wave of popular interest in the new hero quickly swept across Europe and America – indeed, across the globe. A tickertape parade in New York City greeted Lindbergh upon his return. Huge crowds gathered wherever he appeared. Intense press coverage followed. Streets and airports were renamed in his honour. Charles Lindbergh's influence on popular culture would remain for many years.

How the others fared

René Fonck's overloaded plane had crashed on takeoff in 1926. In the weeks following Lindbergh's triumph, Richard Byrd and Clarence Chamberlin also flew the Atlantic. Byrd made it across the Atlantic, but had to ditch his Fokker Trimotor, *America* (below), off the coast of France. All survived. Chamberlin crossed the Atlantic with his sponsor and landed in Berlin, setting a new distance record.

Grim outcome

René Fonck and his copilot survived their horrific crash, but two other crew members were trapped and perished.

So near yet so far

Ditching off the coast of France brought an inglorious end to Richard Byrd's attempt to fly from New York to Paris.

24

A hero's welcome

On 13th June 1927, a huge tickertape parade for Charles Lindbergh was held in New York City. A year later, Lindbergh flew the *Spirit of St. Louis* to all 48 American states, where an estimated 30 million people came out to greet him.

The prize

On 16th June 1927, Raymond Orteig presented Charles Lindbergh with the well-earned winner's check for $25,000 for becoming the first person to fly from New York to Paris.

Lindbergh mania

Buttons, postage stamps, and many other items commemorating Charles Lindbergh's flight were sold in the 1920s.

A lasting legacy

Charles Lindbergh lived a long and active life. He and his wife, Anne, travelled widely to promote commercial aviation. In 1932, tragedy struck when his firstborn son was kidnapped and murdered. In the late 1930s, his views on Nazi Germany and his opposition to war made him unpopular in America, but when World War II broke out he volunteered as a test pilot. Later, he championed environmental causes. He died in 1974.

Brietling Orbiter 3

Bertrand Piccard & Brian Jones

Nonstop Around the World by Balloon

It was high adventure – two daring balloonists seeking aviation's last major record. In March 1999, Bertrand Piccard and Brian Jones flew the *Breitling Orbiter 3* around the world in 19 days, 21 hours, and 55 minutes. Flying above 9,150 m, the pilots faced many challenges, including a temporary loss of cabin oxygen at one point. Their nonstop flight was a high-tech adventure, with an onboard computer, global weather alerts, and a global positioning system (GPS) for navigation. Crucially, they had a talented support team to provide technological and all-important weather advice.

Pilots and friends

Bertrand Piccard (left) is a Swiss psychiatrist and the grandson of famous balloon explorer Auguste Piccard. A former RAF pilot, Briton Brian Jones (right) holds many ballooning records.

Challengers for the record

Between 1981 and 1999, there had been nearly 20 attempts to fly nonstop around the globe by balloon. Some aeronauts, including adventurers Richard Branson, Per Lindstrand, and Steve Fossett, had made repeated attempts, without success. With two failures behind him, Bertrand Piccard knew that the *Breitling Orbiter 3* project was his last chance. Swiss watch company Breitling would not sponsor a fourth flight.

Virgin Global Challenger

Richard Branson and Per Lindstrand launched the *Virgin Global Challenger* from Morocco in 1997, just a week before *Breitling Orbiter 1*. After one day, they were forced down in Algeria as a result of a technical problem.

Breitling Orbiter 1

Flying *Breitling Orbiter 1*, Bertrand Piccard, Wim Verstraeten, and Andy Elson attempted to set the world record in 1997. They had to ditch off Toulon, in France, when kerosene fumes from a leaking valve endangered the crew. All three would try again.

Global Hilton

Also in 1997, Dick Rutan competed for the prize in his *Global Hilton*. Taking off from Albuquerque, New Mexico, Rutan and his partner, Dave Melton, were forced to parachute to safety when a helium cell burst. The balloon was destroyed by fire.

Breitling Orbiter 2

In 1998, Piccard, Verstraeten, and Elson set a world distance record in the *Breitling Orbiter 2* but fell short of circling the globe. Their flight, from Switzerland to Myanmar, took 9 days, 17 hours, and 51 minutes.

Cable & Wireless Balloon

Just days before the *Breitling Orbiter 3* took off, Colin Prescot and Andy Elson launched another challenge in their Cable & Wireless balloon. After 18 days aloft, bad weather forced them to ditch in the Pacific Ocean, off Japan.

Up, Up, and Away!

To accelerate the passage of *Breitling Orbiter 3* across two oceans and three continents, Piccard and Jones planned to attach themselves to powerful winds in the upper atmosphere called jet streams. Flying at high altitudes, the *Orbiter* reached a speed of 370 km/h at times. Keeping the balloon on track required a pilot to be at the controls 24 hours a day; the two balloonists took turns in the pilot's seat. Batteries, regularly recharged by solar energy, supplied internal power. Navigation was aided by GPS positioning and regular weather alerts from the ground control crew. The pilots lived in a van-sized gondola equipped with heating and an elaborate life support system. Most of their food was freeze-dried. As with all past attempts, they knew they would face unknown perils along the way.

Eight-hour shifts

The two pilots took turns working eight-hour shifts in the cockpit, one working while the other slept. To keep on course, they relied on GPS and weather alerts from their ground crew. Communication with the control centre was via a fax transmitter. The *Breitling Orbiter 3* was also fitted with two transponders, allowing air traffic controllers across the globe to track its flight path.

BEAR SAYS

Bertrand Piccard came from a long line of adventurers – his father was an undersea explorer who was one of the first people to explore the Mariana Trench, the deepest place on Earth, and his grandfather was a balloonist.

Final attempt

By the time of the launch, Bertrand Piccard had spent five years on his three *Orbiter* attempts.

Historic moment

In a valley in the Swiss Alps, a crowd gathered to watch the huge *Breitling Orbiter 3* ascend from the village of Château d'Oex (left) at 9:05 am local time on 1st March 1999.

The World's Greatest Balloon Adventure

The story of sport aviation is filled with heroic, record-breaking flights. In 1999, Bertrand Piccard and Brian Jones flew 48,300 km in 19 days to set perhaps the most challenging record of all — the first ever around-the-world flight in a balloon. Balloons are pushed forward by the wind, and pilots have no immediate way to control speed or direction. They can only move the balloon up or down to catch favourable wind patterns. Piccard and Jones used this basic technique on their global adventure: the *Orbiter* ascended into the powerful winds of the jet stream in the upper atmosphere to move across continents and oceans.

BEAR SAYS

Long-distance balloon pilots have to be constantly aware of the amount of propane they have burned while ascending and therefore how many hours' flying they have left.

Up, over, and around the world

After the launch in the Swiss Alps, the pilots flew over Italy and the Mediterranean to Morocco. From there, they travelled east over Africa to the Middle East, then passed over India, southern China, the vast Pacific Ocean, the southwestern United States, and the Atlantic Ocean, finally landing in the Egyptian desert.

Intense cold

Approaching Africa, the *Orbiter* ascended to an altitude of 10,975 m. With an outside temperature well below freezing point, the internal heating system was overwhelmed and the gondola became intensely cold.

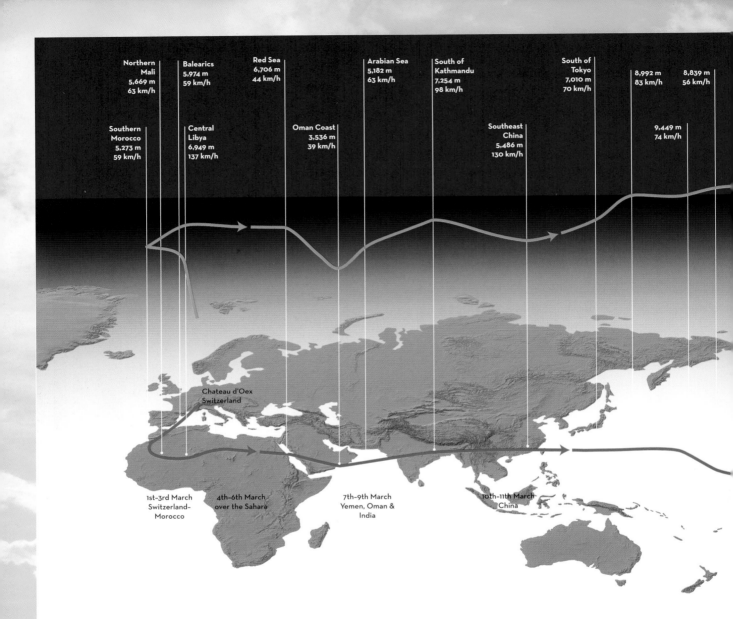

Northern
Mali
5,669 m
63 km/h

Balearics
5,974 m
59 km/h

Red Sea
6,706 m
44 km/h

Arabian Sea
5,182 m
63 km/h

South of
Kathmandu
7,254 m
98 km/h

South of
Tokyo
7,010 m
70 km/h

8,992 m
83 km/h

8,839 m
56 km/h

Southern
Morocco
5,273 m
59 km/h

Central
Libya
6,949 m
137 km/h

Oman Coast
3,536 m
39 km/h

Southeast
China
5,486 m
130 km/h

9,449 m
74 km/h

Chateau d'Oex
Switzerland

1st–3rd March
Switzerland–
Morocco

4th–6th March
over the Sahara

7th–9th March
Yemen, Oman &
India

10th–11th March
China

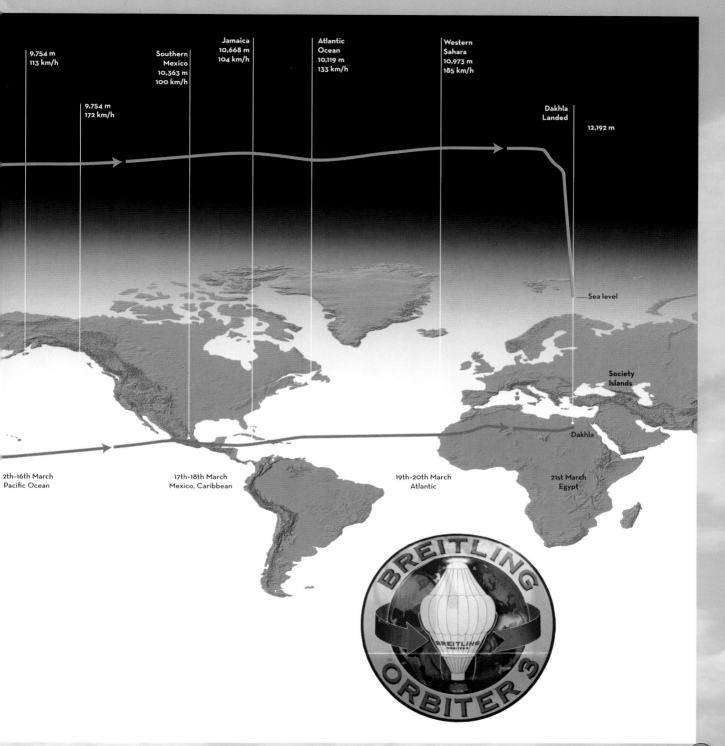

9,754 m
113 km/h

9,754 m
172 km/h

Southern
Mexico
10,363 m
100 km/h

Jamaica
10,668 m
104 km/h

Atlantic
Ocean
10,119 m
133 km/h

Western
Sahara
10,973 m
185 km/h

Dakhla
Landed

12,192 m

Sea level

Society
Islands

Dakhla

2th–16th March
Pacific Ocean

17th–18th March
Mexico, Caribbean

19th–20th March
Atlantic

21st March
Egypt

BREITLING
ORBITER 3
BREITLING
ORBITER 3

A chill in the air

Weather and temperatures are created in a layer of the atmosphere called the troposphere, which extends to about 12,200 m above Earth's surface. In general, as altitudes increase, temperatures decrease. Towards the top of the troposphere, temperatures drop to an average low of −57°C and wind speeds increase significantly.

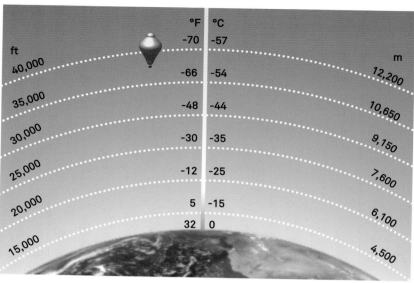

ft	°F	°C	m
40,000	−70	−57	12,200
	−66	−54	10,650
35,000	−48	−44	
30,000	−30	−35	9,150
25,000	−12	−25	7,600
20,000	5	−15	6,100
	32	0	
15,000			4,500

Rocky start

Shortly after the *Breitling Orbiter 3* broke free of its tether at Château d'Oex and ascended, the balloon hit an inversion layer – where cold air at ground level meets the warmer air in the atmosphere – and ceased to climb. The pilots had to act quickly, dumping ballast and igniting the propane burner, to prevent the balloon from drifting and crashing into a mountainside.

View from a space shuttle

A band of cirrus cloud (right) reflects the narrow track of a jet stream moving from left to right across the photograph. This image was taken by a space shuttle an incredible 322 km above Earth.

Catching the jet stream

Jet streams occur at high altitudes and are like "rivers of wind" moving at high speed. They vary between 160–480 km wide and range from 1.6–4.8 km thick. They can reach speeds of up to 724 km/h. Global balloonists aim to catch rides on jet streams to propel them around Earth. A timely jet stream across Africa, predicted by their meteorologists, finally carried Piccard and Jones to Egypt – and success.

A Giant Silver Balloon

The *Breitling Orbiter 3* was a Roziere balloon. This type of balloon flies on a combination of hot air and gas, and is most efficient when the temperature inside the envelope is stabilized as far as possible. The *Orbiter 3* had an outer skin of aluminized Mylar – extending to a height of 55 m when inflated – and a second insulating layer, the "waistcoat". Six propane burners warmed the helium in the gas cell at night, and during the day solar-powered fans reduced heat gain from the Sun by blowing air through the gap between the insulated outer skin and the inner gas cell. The pressurized gondola, with radio, computer, navigation instruments, and other facilities, was the flight's nerve centre.

Life on board

The central part of the pressurized capsule contained a single bunk and a storage area. An ingenious, pressure-operated toilet was screened off with a curtain at the rear of the craft. Burners kept the cabin temperature at 15°C. A water heater was used to warm packets of pre-cooked food and also provided hot water for washing.

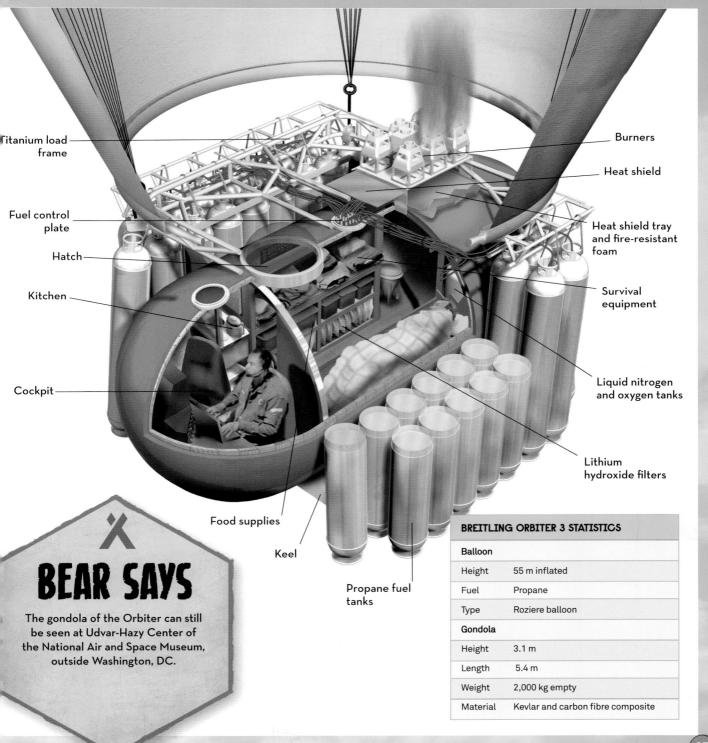

Titanium load frame

Fuel control plate

Hatch

Kitchen

Cockpit

Food supplies

Keel

Burners

Heat shield

Heat shield tray and fire-resistant foam

Survival equipment

Liquid nitrogen and oxygen tanks

Lithium hydroxide filters

Propane fuel tanks

BEAR SAYS

The gondola of the Orbiter can still be seen at Udvar-Hazy Center of the National Air and Space Museum, outside Washington, DC.

BREITLING ORBITER 3 STATISTICS		
Balloon		
Height	55 m inflated	
Fuel	Propane	
Type	Roziere balloon	
Gondola		
Height	3.1 m	
Length	5.4 m	
Weight	2,000 kg empty	
Material	Kevlar and carbon fibre composite	

The first balloons

The observation that smoke rises, and that a paper bag placed over a fire expands and rises, led brothers Joseph and Jacques Montgolfier to invent hot-air balloons. In 1783, they flew the first passengers – a sheep, a rooster, and a duck – in a basket suspended from a hot-air balloon at Versailles, in France, before King Louis XVI and some 130,000 people. The balloon flew nearly 3.2 km. Soon after, Jean-François Pilâtre de Rozier became the first person to fly, staying aloft for four minutes.

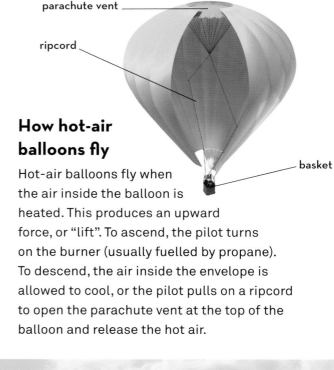

parachute vent

ripcord

basket

How hot-air balloons fly

Hot-air balloons fly when the air inside the balloon is heated. This produces an upward force, or "lift". To ascend, the pilot turns on the burner (usually fuelled by propane). To descend, the air inside the envelope is allowed to cool, or the pilot pulls on a ripcord to open the parachute vent at the top of the balloon and release the hot air.

BEAR SAYS

The hot air balloon is the oldest form of human flight, invented over 100 years before the first aeroplane took off.

How Roziere balloons work

Roziere balloons are named after their inventor, Jean-François Pilâtre de Rozier. De Rozier invented a balloon with two separate chambers, one for a gas with great buoyancy, such as hydrogen, and the other for a "lifting" gas (heated air). Non-flammable helium is now used rather than flammable hydrogen. This type of balloon is suited to long-distance flights, as it consumes less fuel than other balloons.

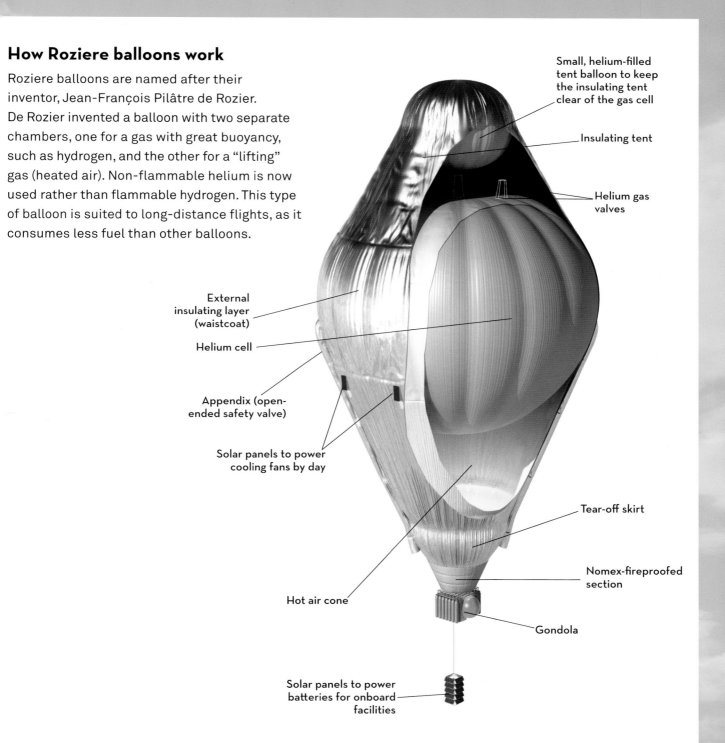

Small, helium-filled tent balloon to keep the insulating tent clear of the gas cell

Insulating tent

Helium gas valves

External insulating layer (waistcoat)

Helium cell

Appendix (open-ended safety valve)

Solar panels to power cooling fans by day

Tear-off skirt

Nomex-fireproofed section

Gondola

Hot air cone

Solar panels to power batteries for onboard facilities

Touchdown in the Desert

At dawn on 21st March, the *Breitling Orbiter 3* began its rapid descent to Earth. The pilots chose the early hours for the critical manoeuvre to avoid the strong winds that occur in the desert during the hot daylight hours. They had passed the finishing line a few hours earlier, over Mauritania, but decided to fly on to Egypt as a safer place to land. Guiding the balloon from the upper atmosphere to ground level was difficult. Suddenly, with a thud, the *Orbiter* made its first contact with Earth as the capsule struck a mass of rocks. The balloon bounced 90 m into the air, then Brian Jones regained control and, after one more tiny bounce, brought it in to land.

Record breakers

Coming in to land, the pilots were elated to know that they had set new world records for distance, duration, and altitude. The *Breitling Orbiter 3* touched down 72 km north of the Egyptian town of Dakhla at 6 am GMT. Less than one tank of fuel remained.

BEAR SAYS

Piccard and Jones inspired many more ballooning records. In 2002, Curtis Rivers bungee jumped from a hot air balloon almost 5 km in the air!

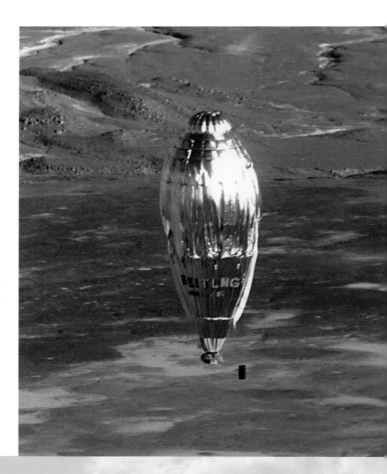

Postscript to a great adventure

During their history-making flight, Bertrand Piccard and Brian Jones reflected on the contrast between their own good fortune and the suffering of many people below them on Earth. On their return, they established the Winds of Hope Foundation, drawing on their media exposure and fundraising potential to combat forgotten or disregarded illnesses and suffering, particularly among children.

Solo around the world

In July 2002, on his sixth attempt, American adventurer Steve Fossett became the first person to fly solo nonstop around the world in a balloon. In his Roziere-type balloon *Spirit of Freedom*, he travelled a total of 32,963 km in 14 days, 19 hours, and 51 minutes.

Bear Grylls

Paramotoring over Everest

I was 23 when I climbed Mount Everest. It was a physically and emotionally life-changing experience, but one I was so proud to achieve, at such a pivotal point in my life, so soon after recovering from a parachuting accident that almost left me unable to walk. At the time, I was one of the youngest climbers to ever summit. It was an ambition I never thought I would top. After all, where else is there to go once you have reached the Roof of the World? Nine years later, I discovered the answer. You go even higher. But I'm not talking about simply flying over Everest in a safe, pressurized, heated commercial aeroplane! No, I wanted to go against the raw elements – the hard way – under a powered paraglider, effectively a parachute with an engine backpack! Nobody had done it before. But Everest was luring me back, with all her dangers, highs, and lows. This turned out to be a challenge unlike anything I had faced before.

Mount Everest – the Roof of the World.

On top of the world

Standing at 8,848 m, Mount Everest is the highest mountain on the planet, located in the Himalaya mountain range. The Nepali locals call it *Sagarmatha*, meaning "the forehead in the sky", or *Chomolungma*, "the mother of the world". At the top, oxygen is so thin that cells in the brain begin to die. They call this the Death Zone.

Journey to the Roof of the World

The first people to summit Everest were New Zealand mountaineer Edmund Hillary and Sherpa Tenzing Norgay (below) in 1953. Many others, myself included, have followed since then – although almost 300 people have perished in the attempt. Many of the bodies still remain there, forever preserved in the ice.

BEAR SAYS

Hillary and Norgay's tale captivated me as a child. I would read about their exploits and dream of one day following in their footsteps. It just goes to show, if you dare to dream, work hard, and never give up, you can achieve anything!

Reach for the skies

So how would we fly to above the height of Mount Everest, using only a small bit of silk and a backpack engine, also called a powered paraglider or paramotor? The main problem was that nobody had ever paramotored at such altitudes before. On top of that, everybody I spoke to said it was impossible. And looking at my options, I was beginning to think so, too.

Gilo Cardozo

Gilo is one of my best buddies and a mega-keen paramotor pilot. He is also a brilliant engineer, and his role was to build the ultimate paramotor, designed for extreme high altitudes. He began tinkering with regular paramotor engines in his Wiltshire workshop. It was his incredible engineering skills that developed a totally unique engine, powerful and lightweight enough to carry us through the hyper thin, oxygen-starved air.

Lethal temperatures

To increase our chances of success, we set out in the late spring when the climbing season opened. Average temperatures on Everest range from −10°C to 10°C, sinking to −30°C in the winter. We were planning to go even higher, in a realm where winds can reach 275 km/h.

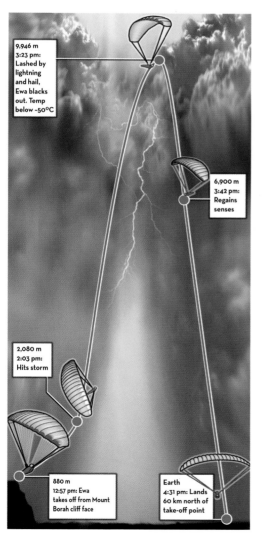

9,946 m
3:23 pm:
Lashed by
lightning
and hail,
Ewa blacks
out. Temp
below −50°C

6,900 m
3:42 pm:
Regains
senses

2,080 m
2:03 pm:
Hits storm

880 m
12:57 pm: Ewa
takes off from Mount
Borah cliff face

Earth
4:31 pm: Lands
60 km north of
take-off point

Turbulance

During a competition in Australia in 2007, German paraglider Ewa Wisnierska (below) was sucked into a storm cloud. She was hauled to 9,946 m, at speeds of 77 km/h, before passing out from lack of oxygen. She flew unconscious for up to an hour, spiralling out of control, before coming round at 6,900 m to the sound of lightning all around her. She landed 3.5 hours later, 60 km from her start position. She was lucky. A fellow competitor was caught in the same storm and killed when lightning struck him.

Ewa Wisnierska's escape was miraculous.

Freefall

Wisnierska's remarkable survival was in large part because of her amazing skill and command of the paraglider. Somebody less experienced probably wouldn't have been so fortunate.

BEAR SAYS

Planning, training, paragliding skills, and good mountain and flying judgement are all essential for a mission like this. My dad had a saying to sum it up: "instinct is the nose of the mind, always trust it".

Preparation

As nobody had done this before, preparation was more critical than ever. Gilo worked for months to perfect a motor that was lightweight, but still powerful enough to carry us. The problem was the higher we soared, the less oxygen the engine had, which meant more fuel would be needed – and fuel was heavy. It was a battle of power vs. weight. On 5th April, with our deadline fast approaching, Gilo and I tested the engine for the first time in a micro-climatic wind tunnel which would simulate the severe temperatures over Everest. Almost immediately, the engine froze and broke.

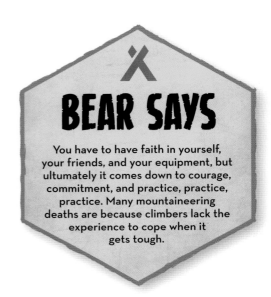

BEAR SAYS

You have to have faith in yourself, your friends, and your equipment, but ultumately it comes down to courage, commitment, and practice, practice, practice. Many mountaineering deaths are because climbers lack the experience to cope when it gets tough.

When testing the strength of aircraft, manufacturers regularly use wind tunnels where they can control the elements. Gilo and I stood inside one, wearing Arctic gear and strapped to our paramotors. It blew us around for over an hour at minus 55°C! I almost suffered from frostbite on my cheeks.

Further preparation

Two days later, we tested the engine for the first time, flying it in the air. Running with the heavy pack, I was finally airborne. It's a thrilling experience, having the ground drift from under your feet. But shortly into the flight, I flew through an area of severe turbulence and my chute's lines became tangled. I dropped like a stone, with the chute only partially inflated. Hitting the ground hard reminded me of the parachute accident that fractured my back. I had almost died on a simple training mission. Was this a sign not to pursue such a dangerous mission? Or simply a reminder to try and train harder?

Out of time

In every mission, timing is critical. With almost no practise in England, our window for travelling to Nepal was rapidly narrowing. And the engines weren't yet fully finished. With precisely zero out of two paramotors working, we had to make a decision whether to continue or postpone the attempt indefinitely. We decided to go for it!

Survival suits

We would wear three separate suits to keep warm: first a thermal layer, then a fire retardant layer in case our engine caught fire, and the last designed to fend off Antarctic temperatures of up to −80°C. Masks pumped a vital stream of oxygen, which could last for 6 hours, while radios in the helmets would keep us in constant communication with our team on the ground, and with each other. Video cameras strapped to the paramotor fed live images, capturing every moment of the adventure.

Our paramotors were fuelled by unleaded petrol. The four-stroke engine pushed us along at about 100 km/h.

Kathmandu

We arrived in Kathmandu, the beautiful capital of Nepal. There was no doubting that it was good to be back in the mighty Himalayas, but I don't mind admitting that the excitement was also heavily tinged with fear. The paramotors were still untested, and the weather forecast for the week ahead made for grim reading.

Namche Bazaar

Hopping on a big, old, Russian helicopter, we landed at Namche Bazaar (3,400 m), also known as the Sherpa capital, where we were joined by our team of Sherpas, who would help carry our equipment into the heart of these giant mountains. These men knew every inch of the mountains, and it was wonderful to

Kathmandu, Nepal

spend time with them on the three-day trek to our basecamp. I recall the look of terror and amazement on Gilo's face when he first set eyes upon Everest in the distance. It reminded me of the first time I had seen her. But with this new endeavour in mind, that climb seemed like a lifetime ago. As we finally reached the village of Pheriche, which, at 4,400 m, would serve as our basecamp, the weather took a turn for the worst, reminding us all who was really in charge out here – Mother Nature.

Namche Bazaar

Basecamp

We spent three days essentially snowed into our tents, where even resting was uncomfortable due to the thin air, with only 60% of oxygen available to us at that altitude. We needed to make some test flights before the big attempt at Everest, but Mother Nature was denying us such opportunities. At times like this, your resolve is tested. When you are nervous, being forced to wait can sometimes be the hardest thing, yet all we could do was sit and watch the ever-deteriorating weather reports.

CHINA

NEPAL

▲ Mount Everest

■ KATHMANDU

INDIA

0 — 50 km
0 — 50 mi

The team

Gilo and I had assembled an experienced group around us. Our 13-strong team included medics, weather experts, radio operators, and other experienced paragliders. We even had a TV crew documenting the expedition. It was overseen by our safety expert, Neil Laughton. Neil had been my climbing buddy on Everest many years before, and I trusted his opinion 100%. I know I can be too impulsive and keen to press on with an adventure, but Neil is far more thoughtful and will rein me in when the risk is too high. Having him on this expedition probably saved my life, when he persuaded us to wait for better weather.

Acclimatization

While sitting around and waiting was not good for the mind, it was essential for the body. Breathing is difficult at these altitudes, and even the smallest activity becomes an arduous task that can leave you gasping for breath. Pushing your body too hard can be deadly, so it's important to allow your body to get used to these conditions. This process is called acclimatization.

The great British explorer, Sir Ranulph Fiennes, lost his fingertips from severe frostbite – when your skin freezes.

Altitude sickness

Invisible dangers are always the worst. Up here, it's the dreaded signs of altitude sickness that you must be vigilant for. It may start out as a slight headache or light-headedness. Perhaps you simply have difficulty sleeping. Loss of appetite, trouble breathing, and vomiting are also common symptoms. If ignored, this can lead to pulmonary or cerebral edema. And that means death.

Day Four

Unpredictable weather means that clear periods come about just as suddenly as foul ones. Quite unexpectedly, the skies turned blue and I was eager to be away. However, it wasn't as simple as strapping the paramotor pack on and setting off. First, the medical team attached sensors to monitor our vital signs. A weather balloon had to be sent up to test for high winds around us, and cameras had to be attached to the paramotor frames to record our adventure for a Channel 4 and Discovery Channel documentary. All of that takes time. In total, we would have to carry and run with a total take-off weight of 75 kg of equipment – and Gilo still hadn't flown his pack at all!

Preparing to fly a Paramotor

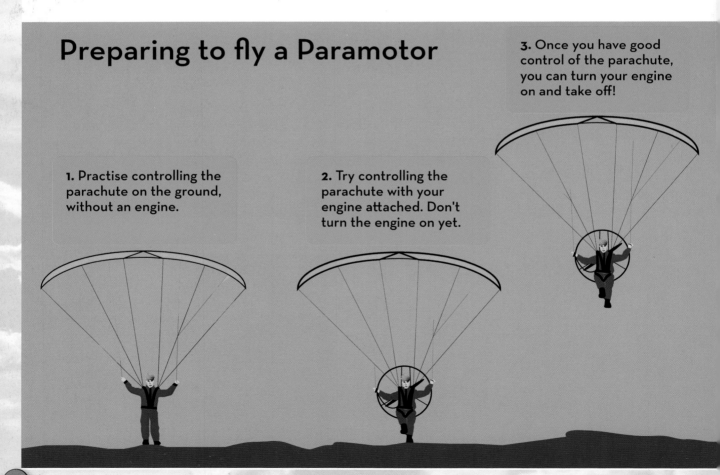

1. Practise controlling the parachute on the ground, without an engine.

2. Try controlling the parachute with your engine attached. Don't turn the engine on yet.

3. Once you have good control of the parachute, you can turn your engine on and take off!

Storm clouds rolling in over the Himalayas can turn day into night. The last place you want to be is in the air.

Out of time

The weather window was closing, and by 7:30 am clouds were already mustering at the lofty peaks around us. The tech teams worked as quickly as they could and sent up a weather balloon to gain better wind speed readings – but the computer failed to make a data connection. With the clock ticking, it was almost another hour before the weather data came in. By then, we could already see the clouds encroaching all around us...

Abort!

When you're pumped up with adrenaline, there's nothing you want to do more than just go. I could see the clouds, but was convinced we could take flight and be down before they hit. Gilo decided it was too dangerous to go. But despite my better judgement, I was still keen to give it a go. It eventually took a firm decision from Neil to abort the mission to settle the matter. Gilo and Neil were both proved right.

BEAR SAYS

Having a trusted friend oversee dangerous expeditions is a wise move. It's all too easy to become too focused on the goal – and not on the signs and dangers around you!

Day Five

After being snowed in for three days, and the aborted attempt on the fourth day, I had a fitful night's sleep. My worry was that another window in the weather may not open up for weeks, if at all this season. But when is worrying ever helpful? As we awoke the following morning, we were greeted by perfect weather. I felt it was a gift from the mountain! Suddenly, it was all systems go!

BEAR SAYS

Even in these freezing conditions, warm air currents race around the peaks. These columns of warm air lift you up and spit you out. They can be very violent. They're also invisible, so you have to be on high alert to avoid being thrown into the side of a mountain!

Ready!

Remembering the previous day, I focused on remaining calm as the team scrambled to get the equipment ready. We could clearly see Everest beckoning, a giant above us. However, with all the waiting around came the doubts, remembering comments from those who thought we were attempting the impossible. Andy Elson, the first man to fly over Everest in a balloon, had put our chances of failure at 70%. So I tried to focus everything on that 30% chance of success!

The calm before the storm

On any mission, it's important to take a moment and calm yourself. There will be plenty of time for adrenaline later.

The view as I soared into the air was breathtaking.

Stalled

This was it... we were ready to go. I could feel my heart pounding in my chest in anticipation. Then came the news I didn't want to hear – Gilo's engine wouldn't fire up. It took almost 90 minutes for him to fix the problem, against all the odds. All the while, I kept a wary eye on the clouds...

Go!

The call came from Neil – go! I ran forward... but almost immediately fell over under the huge weight! This happened three times. The size of the engine, all the equipment, and the sheer scale of this huge, oversized parachute meant launching was an impossibly cumbersome process. I was getting so tired. I didn't think I could go on. My heart rate was up at 160 beats per minute, through exertion, exhaustion, and fear. But I was determined to go again. I told myself never to give up. Finally, at 8:21 am, I finally made it into the air...

Cliff!

As soon as I was in the air I struggled to get control of the machine as I headed straight towards a cliff! Luckily, I was able to turn away at the last minute.

Airborne!

Seeing that I was now in control of the paramotor, Gilo sprang into the air nine minutes later. We were all very much aware that it was the first time he had flown with the pack. However, a quick glance around confirmed my friend was safely in the air. The deep blue skies above us beckoned us onwards and upwards. It looked like we were going to get a chance to complete the mission after all!

Active piloting

"Active piloting" is the term used to control the wing — in this case, the wing was twice the normal size to be able to keep us airborne in such thin air at the extreme altitude. It's not as simple as sitting back and admiring the view, it requires constant attention to keep the wing flying and avoid it collapsing in the tubulence.

Free as a bird

At this moment in time, Gilo and I were kings of the sky! The constant buzz from the engine vibrated through our bones, but it assured us that everything was running smoothly. We were rewarded with an incredible view of the Himalayas. And still we continued to ascend...

At 7,000 m and climbing, there weren't even any birds as high as us.

BEAR SAYS

"Be prepared" is the motto of the Scouts – and, as Chief Scout, I can assure you it's probably the best piece of advice any of us will ever receive.

The Roof of the World

The world record for a paramotor climb was 7,589 m, which we would have to beat to soar over the world's highest peak. I kept getting glimpses of the chopper being used by the film crew and felt a glimmer of satisfaction that it would be unable to climb above 6,700 m – and we'd soon be above it!

Ready for anything

Any risky venture should always have a plan B, and Neil had ensured we did too. Aside from the thermal suits and fighter pilot-like helmets, we carried survival kits. Looking between my feet as the Himalayas rolled by, I was most thankful for the skydiving rig. In case of fire, or if my main wing collapsed and was unrecoverable, this could save my life.

Survival kit

Neil had insisted we carry a survival bag containing food, water, mini-flares, and emergency locator beacons... just in case. However, the reality was if we crashed into Everest, there would be little chance of rescue, and our survival would only be a matter of hours at such high altitude and in low temperatures.

Tech Problems

When things go wrong, they appear to do so in rapid succession, like dominoes falling. I felt the first ripples of fear in my stomach when the radio communications started to become garbled and unintelligible. Without a working radio, the ground crew wouldn't be able to warn us of fast-approaching weather, or if we were drifting off target. At 6,700 m, I started to feel very isolated indeed.

Comms down

Clear communications are vital, and have been the Achilles' heel of many an expedition.

Click if you can hear us

Keeping a clear head in any crisis is vital. I may have had trouble hearing the ground crew, but I could clearly see I was on course for Everest, and a quick check around assured me there were no sneaky storm clouds trying to muscle their way in. Plus, Gilo was still by my side. So far, so good. In the garbled messages from our ground crew, I could just about hear Neil repeating his system – three rapid clicks on the radio mic for yes, two for no. "Are we still good to proceed?" he asked. I clicked once, twice, three times.

The peak border

The peak of Everest is one of the most iconic border markers in the world, as it's exactly split between Nepal and Chinese-controlled Tibet.

China

Now, with just the buzz of the engine and the roaring wind to distract me, I focused on my target ahead. We only had a permit to fly on the south side of Everest – the Nepalese side. As the wind buffeted my tiny parachute, my arms began to ache from wrestling for control. It was vital to stay on target and not drift over to the north side of the mountain and into Chinese airspace and turbulent rotor wind conditions.

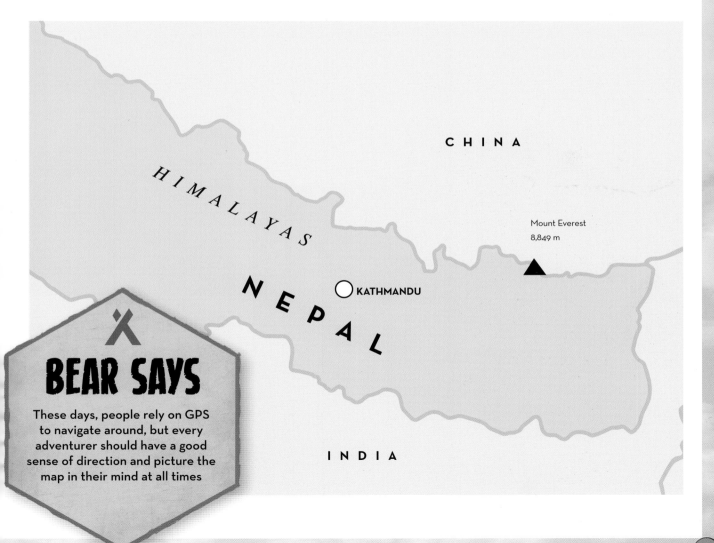

CHINA

HIMALAYAS

NEPAL

○ KATHMANDU

Mount Everest
8,849 m

INDIA

BEAR SAYS

These days, people rely on GPS to navigate around, but every adventurer should have a good sense of direction and picture the map in their mind at all times

Man Down!

At 6,900 m, with Everest to one side, I was still climbing and the views were becoming increasingly more stunning. The moment was suddenly punctured by a garbled message over the radio bringing more bad news. Gilo had developed engine trouble. It was difficult for me to see what was happening, but I knew this was the risk of not having time to finish testing the engines back in England.

While they may be beautiful, the Himalayas are not somewhere you want to be stranded.

Engine fault

Gilo knew his engines inside out and back to front. Only 2,000 m below the peak, he was able to diagnose the problem. His crackling radio message told us the supercharger belt had failed. Despite his craftsmanship, the intense cold still managed to claw its way into the engine to cause the damage. He had perfected one engine and had selflessly given it to me, without me knowing. That's a true friend for you.

Alone

I could do nothing but watch as Gilo slowly spiralled back to Earth. I knew being defeated by a technical failure would be tough for him, but at least he was safe. Using our click-system, I assured Neil that I was good to continue. I gave a quick nod to the on-board camera and climbed as the fierce winds continued to gain strength. Strong winds are a constant factor at the summit and could easily rip apart my parachute if I got caught out.

My helmet camera was able to record the amazing vista ahead.

Cresting the Peak

The paramotor engine strained as winds of up to 120 km/h walloped into me. The outside temperature was sinking to −80°C, but I pressed on. Gilo was down by now, and the camera helicopter was well below, unable to catch me. Very slowly, Everest's peak, the very place I had stood nine years earlier, drew to eye level... then dropped beneath me.

On top of the world

Without my buddy by my side, I felt so vulnerable up there. By this point, I must be nothing more than a tiny speck in the sky to those on the ground. My feelings of fear soon evaporated, though, when I realised I had a heavenly view: Nepal and China stretched out around me; the highest peaks in the world now mere blips beneath my feet. It's an image that will stay with me forever.

Mission accomplished

At about 8,990 m, the engine finally cut out in the thin air, and I was rewarded with blessed near-silence. Only the wind slicing across me could be heard. I was higher than any other paramotor had ever been. Now there was nothing to do except keep the parachute flying safely and treasure the amazing vista as I glided back down to Earth.

Without a bump

Many experts had told us that trying to land such a heavy paramotor at over 4,500 m with so much gear would break our legs. As the ground approached, I was so nervous. But at the last minute, a gentle valley breeze picked up, which slowed my descent perfectly. At 10:11 am, I touched down in a small village about a mile from basecamp. No matter how awe-inspiring the view had been, there was no denying my relief at having solid ground beneath my feet once again. Only then did the elation come – we had done it! I had soared higher than Everest in a paramotor and lived to tell the tale. Mission complete, and what a testament to Gilo's engineering, skill, and selflessness.

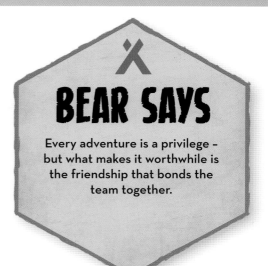

BEAR SAYS

Every adventure is a privilege - but what makes it worthwhile is the friendship that bonds the team together.

Teamwork

It was so tough that Gilo had to turn back, but it was his incredible creation that allowed me to complete our goal. That is the real spirit of a team adventure!

To the team on the ground, I was little more than a tiny, white speck in the sky.

Apollo 11

Neil Armstrong, Buzz Aldrin & Michael Collins

The Moon and Earth

Our nearest celestial body, the Moon, has always fascinated people. In prehistoric times, people marvelled at the mysterious object in the sky that could change its shape, disappear, and then return again. It was only natural that people associated the Moon with divine or magical powers. Ancient sky-watchers learned to calculate time by following the lunar phases. In time, people discovered that the Moon controlled the tides. With the invention of the telescope, observers could see the lunar surface for the first time – a realm of rugged mountains and volcanic plains. Over the centuries, the Moon has inspired poetry, songs, and myths. Yet, one thought lingered in people's minds – how could we travel to this heavenly body? The realization of this dream, the ultimate journey of exploration, finally became possible in the 20th century thanks to the invention of the rocket.

Dawn of the Space Age

In the early 1900s, pioneers like Konstantin Tsiolkovsky, Hermann Oberth, and Robert Goddard experimented with rockets. During World War II, Wernher von Braun launched Nazi Germany's V-2 rocket to the edge of space. The V-2 was developed as a missile, but after the war, interest grew in its potential for space exploration.

Rocket pioneer

American physicist Robert Goddard (above) designed and flew the world's first successful liquid-fuelled rocket. Launched on 16th March 1926, it flew 12.5 m in 2.5 seconds.

Forever famous

Astronauts Neil Armstrong, Michael Collins, and Edwin "Buzz" Aldrin completed the first manned lunar landing in July 1969.

Apollo 7
October 1968
The first manned Apollo flight, with crew members Walter Schirra, Walter Cunningham, and Donn Eisele, lasted 10 days, 20 hours, and 9 minutes.

Apollo 8
December 1968
Frank Borman, James Lovell, and William Anders travelled from Earth to the Moon and returned safely – a flight of 6 days and 3 hours.

Apollo 9
March 1969
This critical mission to practice docking with the Lunar Module was flown by James McDivitt, David Scott, and Russell Schweickart.

Apollo 10
May 1969
Thomas Stafford, Eugene Cernan, and John Young descended to within 22 km of the lunar surface in the last critical test before a historic Moon landing.

Apollo 11
July 1969
NASA astronauts Neil Armstrong, Edwin "Buzz" Aldrin, and Michael Collins made the first successful Moon landing.

Firsts in Space

The Space Age arrived dramatically on 4th October 1957, when the Soviet Union launched Sputnik into Earth orbit. The world's first artificial satellite, Sputnik sent back radio signals, or "beeps", to an awestruck world below. In 1961, Russian cosmonaut Yuri Gagarin became the first person to orbit the Earth. Throughout the 1960s, the Soviet Union and the United States competed with each other, launching satellites and robotic space probes, performing space walks, and developing powerful rockets. One major prize remained to be claimed – a manned mission to the Moon.

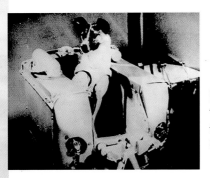

Sputnik 1

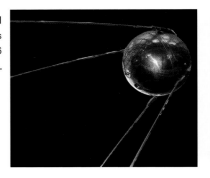

A silver ball with four antennae, the first Sputnik was launched in October 1957. It weighed 83 kg and took 96 minutes to complete its first orbit.

Pioneer in space

The first animal to fly in space was a dog named Laika, the sole passenger on Russia's Sputnik 2 (1957). Unfortunately, there was no way to return her to Earth.

Ham the chimp

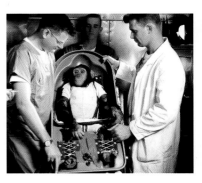

In January 1961, NASA launched a chimpanzee named Ham into a suborbital flight to test the physical hazards of space before the first American went into orbit. Ham was returned safely.

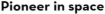

Gagarin the bold

Amid great secrecy, Russian Yuri Gagarin rode a powerful R-7 rocket into orbit in 1961. The world looked on in disbelief as the young cosmonaut flew 303 km into space.

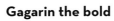

Space walk hero

In 1962, Russian Aleksei Leonov made the first space walk. He overcame many challenges on this high-risk mission, including a malfunctioning spacesuit, which inflated in the vacuum of space, making it difficult for him to get back through the airlock. Luckily, he used his intuition to open a valve in the suit, releasing some of the pressure and allowing him to return to his capsule safely.

Apollo 8 computer technology

The crucial task assigned to the onboard Apollo Guidance Computer (AGC) was to calculate the relative position of the spacecraft to Earth and the Moon. The AGC weighed 32 kg and was housed in a wooden box. It was slow and cumbersome, consuming less energy than a 60 watt light bulb. Though primitive by today's standards, it programmed the long flight path to the Moon and back accurately. The AGC was equipped with a small processor and read-only memory. Most of today's desktop computers have a processor speed 1,000 times faster.

Apollo 8: man around the Moon

The Apollo 8 mission of 1968 was a bold and courageous undertaking. Bolting out of Earth orbit, astronauts Frank Borman, James Lovell, and William Anders travelled 381,500 km to reach the Moon. No one had ever travelled so far from Earth. Everyone knew that any failure of the Saturn rocket would mean isolation and death in deep space. The Apollo 8 crew observed the Moon from a dramatic vantage point a mere 112 km above the lunar surface. Their cameras also glanced backwards to capture stunning images of the now distant planet Earth, prompting a new appreciation of Earth's beauty. Apollo 8 pointed to a future lunar landing.

The First Moon Landing

The bold vision of Apollo 11 was to land astronauts on the Moon and return them safely to Earth. Some 76 hours into the mission, the Apollo 11 spacecraft entered into lunar orbit. Neil Armstrong and Edwin "Buzz" Aldrin then descended in the Lunar Module, *Eagle,* for their historic Moon landing, while Michael Collins continued in orbit at the controls of the Command and Service Module, *Columbia*. The high-risk landing on the Sea of Tranquility took place at 4:18 pm eastern daylight time on 20th July 1969. A camera aboard the *Eagle* provided live television coverage of Armstrong's first step onto the Moon, at 10:56 pm. The astronauts explored the airless and desolate lunar surface for nearly 2.5 hours. Once back on board the *Columbia*, they jettisoned the *Eagle* and rocketed home, landing in the Pacific Ocean.

Preparing for orbit

The Apollo 11 crew underwent rigorous training. They practised every single step of the Moon landing beforehand, from planting the American flag on the surface of the Moon to simulating their return to Earth by dropping a replica lunar module into a swimming pool!

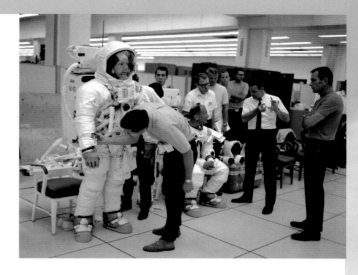

All hands on deck

Every console in the Kennedy Space Flight Center was occupied for the historic launch countdown, and the NASA Mission Control staff erupted into applause as the Apollo 11 crew lifted off.

Watching history

The launch of Apollo 11 was watched on television by millions of people all around the world. Apollo's Saturn rockets were packed with so much fuel that the VIP spectators who watched the launch had to stand over 5 km away in case the rockets exploded.

A New World

As the world looked on, Neil Armstrong and Edwin "Buzz" Aldrin explored this desolate, atmosphere-free realm. They reported that the surface looked like bright daylight against the backdrop of a pitch-black sky. The horizon appeared close and beckoning. The moonscape itself appeared tan in colour, with small and large boulders strewn about. For the visitors from Earth, motion was effortless yet awkward in the one-sixth gravity of the Moon. Footprints left a distinct impression in the powdery surface. The astronauts spent nearly 2.5 hours outside the *Eagle*, planting the American flag, setting up scientific experiments, taking photographs, and collecting sample rocks. Above, in lunar orbit, Michael Collins took photographs of the rugged and forbidding highlands of the Moon's far side.

Live from the Moon

Neil Armstrong's first step onto the Moon represented the fulfillment of an ancient dream. "The Moon had been awaiting us for a long time", Armstrong said later.

Magnificent desolation

"Beautiful, beautiful ... magnificent desolation" were the words Buzz Aldrin used to describe the lunar landscape. Parked on the rugged surface of the Moon, the *Eagle* was an alien visitor.

Moon rocks

NASA eagerly awaited the return of Apollo 11 to examine sample rocks removed from the lunar surface. The rocks proved to be a scientific treasure trove. Careful analysis of the samples revealed much about the history of the Moon over four billion years. Currently, the rocks are housed in the Johnson Space Center, Houston, Texas.

For all humankind

Early in the moonwalk, Neil Armstrong and Buzz Aldrin planted the American flag on the lunar soil (left). This act was not a claim of ownership, but symbolized a proud American achievement in space exploration.

BEAR SAYS

Planting the flag was much harder than it looked. The surface of the Moon was a thin layer of dust over hard rock, so the astronauts had to be careful not to knock it over.

Footprint for posterity

Buzz Aldrin's photograph of his footprint in the lunar soil (left) became one of the most famous images ever taken, a symbol of the human urge to explore.

Space-suited

Portable life support system
This backpack supplied oxygen, regulated the spacesuit temperature, and contained the radios and antennae for communication.

Visor
A visor coated with a thin layer of gold shielded against sunburn from the intense UltraViolet light.

Heartbeat
Sensors recorded the astronaut's heart rate and oxygen consumption. The data was relayed to a doctor at Mission Control.

Safety seal
The heart of the spacesuit was the pressure garment assembly. It formed an airtight seal against the vacuum of space.

Urine collection and transfer
The contents of this bag were emptied into a waste fluid container in the Lunar Module.

Undergarment
The layer against the skin was lined with tubes of flowing water to keep the astronaut cool.

First defense
The white outermost layer protected the astronaut from solar radiation and micrometeoroids.

Moonboots
The lunar boots were slipped on over the inner boots of the pressure garment assembly. They had ribbed silicon rubber soles.

Man on the Moon

The Apollo 11 mission was one of the defining achievements of the 20th century. On 16th July 1969, NASA astronauts Neil Armstrong, Michael Collins, and Edwin "Buzz" Aldrin took off from the Kennedy Space Center in Florida. On 19th July, the Apollo 11 spacecraft entered lunar orbit. The Command and Lunar Modules separated, and the Lunar Module *Eagle*, with Armstrong and Aldrin on board, landed on the lunar surface. Neil Armstrong then took the historic first step onto the Moon.

Saturn V rocket

In the nine minutes it took for the *Saturn V* rocket to climb into space, it burned up enough liquid fuel and enough liquid oxygen to fill one-and-a-half Olympic-sized swimming pools. Its force was powerful enough to lift 500 elephants off the ground. Yet, despite its towering size, at the end of the Apollo 11 mission only the Command Module, with the astronauts on board, returned intact to Earth.

Launch escape tower
This solid-fuel rocket could lift the Command Module away from *Saturn V* in an emergency. (It was not used).

Command Module
The three astronauts lived and worked here during their journey to and from the Moon.

Service Module
This supplied the Command Module with oxygen, electricity, and rocket power. It was jettisoned just before re-entry into Earth's atmosphere.

Lunar Module
The Lunar Module was tucked away above the top S-IVB stage for launch. It was pulled free by the Command Module once in space.

S-IVB third stage
This single-engine stage was used to propel the Apollo 11 spacecraft away from Earth orbit and towards the Moon.

S-IC fuel tank
Kerosene was the main fuel. When it was burned with liquid oxygen, superhot exhaust gases propelled the rocket upward.

S-II second stage
The second stage fired for six minutes, boosting the third stage and the Apollo spacecraft to an altitude of 183 km.

Interstage
The three rocket stages were connected by structures called interstages. When the stages separated, they broke away and fell back to Earth.

S-IC LOX tank
Cold liquid oxygen (LOX) allowed the liquid kerosene fuel to burn even in the near-vacuum of space.

S-IC first stage
The first stage fired for two-and-a -half minutes, boosting the upper stages and the Apollo spacecraft to an altitude of 61 km.

Fuel tank
Flammable fuel or liquid oxygen was held in an insulated tank to keep these super-cold liquids from turning to gas.

Getting there and back

The system NASA chose for the Apollo 11 lunar landing employed two specialized spacecraft: one that orbited the Moon and returned to Earth – the Command and Service Module, named *Columbia* – and a small second craft that landed on and lifted off from the Moon – the Lunar Module, named *Eagle*. Each carried exactly the amount of rocket fuel needed for the task, which allowed the size and cost of each craft to be kept as low as possible. The high-tech sequence of events involved in getting to the Moon, landing, and returning safely to planet Earth is shown in detail below

Leaving Earth

1 Liftoff
The three-stage *Saturn V* rocket, with the Command, Service, and Lunar Modules on top, takes off from the Kennedy Space Center, placing the craft and crew into orbit around Earth.

2 Translunar injection
The first and second stages of *Saturn V* fall back to Earth. After one orbit of Earth, the third-stage engine fires to propel the spacecraft toward the Moon.

3 Transposition and docking
The crew detach the combined Command and Service Module, turn it around, then pull the Lunar Module from the third stage. The discarded third stage goes on to hit the Moon.

Lunar arrival

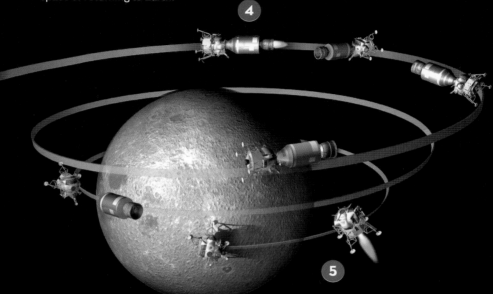

4 Lunar orbit insertion
Three days later, the Service Module's main engine slows down the Apollo 11 craft so that it enters into orbit around the Moon instead of flying off into space or returning to Earth.

5 Descent to the moon
The Lunar Module, with Armstrong and Aldrin on board, separates and lands on the Moon, leaving Michael Collins in orbit in the Command and Service Module.

BEAR SAYS

Neil Armstrong and Buzz Aldrin commented on the weird smell of Moon dust – the 4 billion year old dust apparently gave off a smell like gunpowder!

Leaving the Moon

8 Transearth injection
With all three astronauts on board the Command Module, the Service Module's main engine fires again to power the craft away from the Moon and back toward Earth for the three-day journey home.

7 Re-docking in lunar orbit
The ascent stage of the Lunar Module re-docks with the Command Module. The three astronauts are reunited. The ascent stage is then discarded and hits the Moon.

6 Ascent stage liftoff
After exploring the Moon, Armstrong and Aldrin return to the top half of the Lunar Module. This ascent stage has its own rocket and blasts off the Moon. The bottom half is left behind.

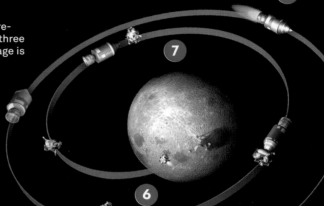

Returning to Earth

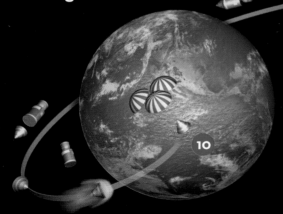

10 Splashdown
The Command Module falls through the atmosphere, and three parachutes open to slow its descent. The craft splashes down in the Pacific Ocean, where a helicopter picks up the crew.

9 Re-entry
On reaching the Earth's atmosphere, the Command Module separates from the Service Module. Both re-enter, but only the Command Module survives, protected by its heat shield.

Lunar Module

Landing on the Moon required a special spacecraft. As the Moon has no air, the Lunar Module did not need to be aerodynamic. Its shape was dictated by the items it was to carry or house: rocket engines, fuel tanks, and a pressurized compartment for two astronauts. It had two parts: the lower descent stage contained the legs, the fuel tanks, and the rocket engine for landing on the Moon. It also stored tools and experiment packages. The ascent stage had its own rocket engine and used the descent stage as a launch pad, blasting off to return the astronauts to the Command and Service Module.

Command and Service Module

The main Apollo 11 spacecraft consisted of two parts: a cone-shaped Command Module attached to a cylindrical Service Module. The Command Module was where the three astronauts lived for most of the mission. The Service Module contained a rocket that fired once to slow the craft and place it into orbit around the Moon, and again to boost it out of lunar orbit and back to Earth. The Command Module was the only portion of the spacecraft to return to Earth.

Propellant tanks
These large tanks stored fuel for the Service Module's main engine.

Engine nozzle
The main rocket was fired when entering and leaving lunar orbit and occasionally for mid-course corrections.

BEAR SAYS

Though the American flag was famously planted on the lunar surface, it was actually blown away when the Lunar Module took off!

Deep-space antenna
This four-dish antenna was used to communicate with Earth.

Oxygen and hydrogen tanks
Gases in these tanks supplied air for the crew and generated electricity.

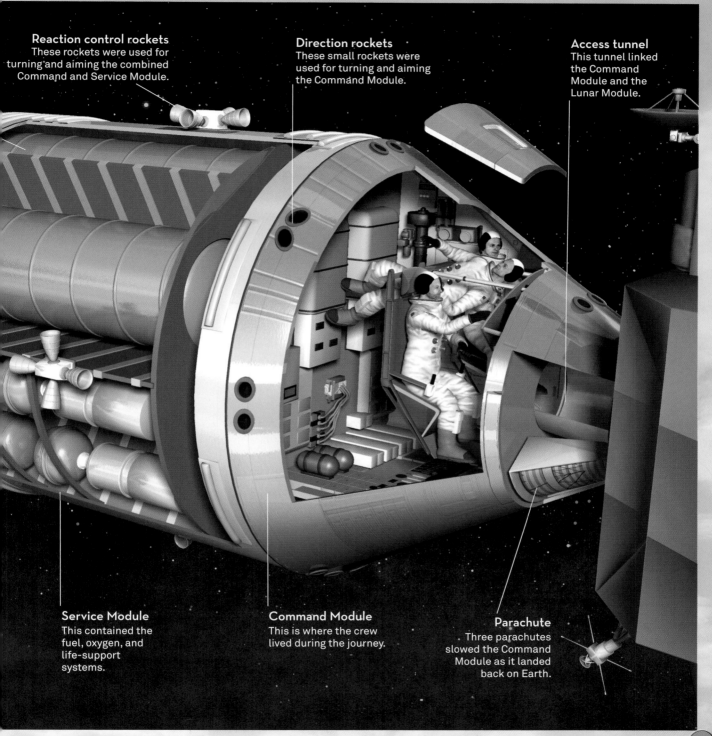

Reaction control rockets
These rockets were used for turning and aiming the combined Command and Service Module.

Direction rockets
These small rockets were used for turning and aiming the Command Module.

Access tunnel
This tunnel linked the Command Module and the Lunar Module.

Service Module
This contained the fuel, oxygen, and life-support systems.

Command Module
This is where the crew lived during the journey.

Parachute
Three parachutes slowed the Command Module as it landed back on Earth.

Mission Accomplished

Once they were reunited in the cocoon of the Apollo 11 Command Module, the three astronauts headed home, a journey of nearly 400,000 km across the void of space. Splashdown in the Pacific Ocean signalled the end of this awe-inspiring adventure. For the first time, Earthlings had left their home and boldly set foot on the surface of another celestial body. Many visionaries dreamed of future exploratory trips to Mars and beyond. Seeing Earth from the Moon, a tiny blue planet in the vast expanse of space, gave people all over the world a new sense of the universe and of our place in it. With the success of the Apollo 11 mission, the objective set by President John F. Kennedy in 1961, to land men on the Moon and return them safely to Earth before the end of the decade, had been accomplished. The story persists as one of the most heroic episodes in the saga of human exploration.

Splashdown

Three parachutes slowed the descent of the Apollo 11 during the splashdown maneuver. As the capsule hit the water, balloons inflated to keep it upright. Navy divers then rescued the crew. The retrieval of the capsule and crew was a highly rehearsed manoeuvre.

In quarantine

Safely aboard the carrier *Hornet*, the Apollo 11 astronauts were placed in a sealed stainless steel trailer called the Mobile Quarantine Facility to protect Earth from potential contamination from the Moon.

Falcon Heavy

Space travel has come a long way since the first person set foot on the moon. In 2018, Elon Musk's company SpaceX sent *Falcon Heavy* into orbit, a partially-reusable rocket that can return to Earth after takeoff. Eventually, the plan is to use this to send humans as far as Mars, but on its first launch it carried a different payload into space – a bright red Tesla Roadster, playing David Bowie's *Life on Mars* on the radio!

Gipsy Moth *Jason*

Amy Johnson

Solo to Australia

In 1930, with a newly minted pilot's license and just 85 hours' experience in the cockpit, a bold young Englishwoman named Amy Johnson flew solo from London to Australia. Air enthusiasts were awestruck. The unknown young pilot had flown her small Gipsy Moth biplane across Europe, the Middle East, India, Burma (Myanmar), Singapore, and the Dutch East Indies (Indonesia) to Darwin. She did not beat Bert Hinkler's record, as she set out to do, but her flight was full of drama and set a new benchmark for women in aviation. Alongside Amelia Earhart, Amy Johnson emerged as one of the most famous female aviators of the 1930s.

Famous duo

Amy Johnson named her Gipsy Moth biplane *Jason*. A sport plane powered by a liquid-cooled engine, it typically cruised at 137 km/h, and with a full tank could fly 515 km.

Bert Hinkler

In 1928, Australian pilot Bert Hinkler (left) became a global celebrity when he flew his Avro Avian biplane from England to Australia in 15.5 days – a remarkable feat for the time. Amy Johnson had hoped to break his record. Hinkler was a national hero in Australia, having flown in World War I with the Royal Naval Air Service. He perished in an air accident in Italy in 1933.

1919

Australian brothers Ross and Keith Smith completed the first England-to-Australia flight within 30 days, winning a $10,000 prize offered by the Australian government.

1920

Flying a single-engine De Havilland DH9 biplane, Australian pilots Raymond Parer and John McIntosh made a mammoth 208-day, accident-filled flight from London to Australia.

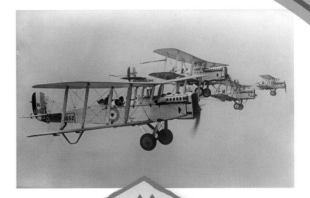

BEAR SAYS

It took nearly 50 years for the first passenger plane to complete a non-stop flight from Australia to London. In 1989, David Massey-Greene flew a Boeing 747-400 on a journey that took almost 20 hours!

1928

Australian Charles Kingsford Smith and his two-man crew made the first trans-Pacific flight, from San Francisco to Brisbane, in an open-cockpit Fokker Trimotor.

1928

Bert Hinkler made the first solo flight from England to Australia. Hinkler also set a new record, completing the journey in 15.5 days.

1930

Charles Kingsford Smith flew solo from London to Australia in 9 days and 22 hours, breaking Bert Hinkler's record by just over 5.5 days.

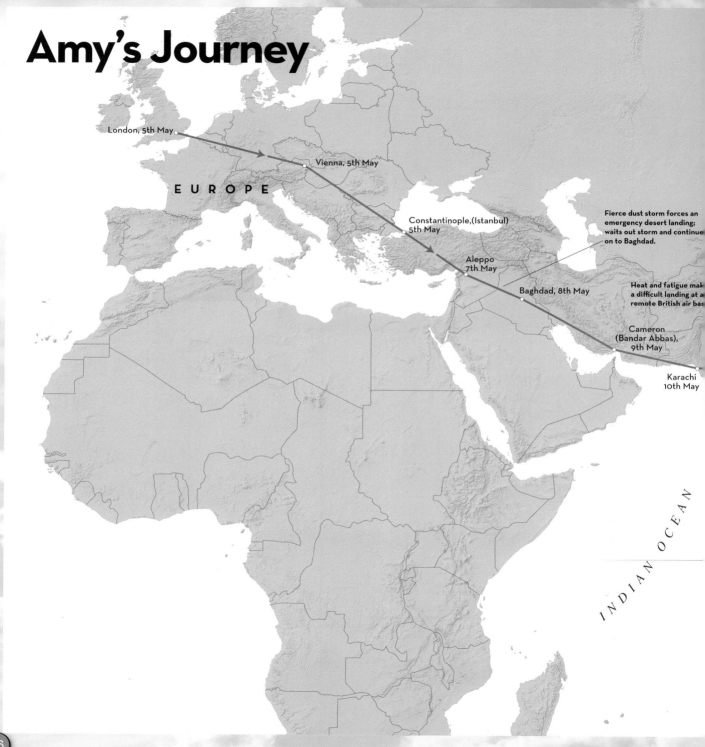

Amy's Journey

EUROPE

London, 5th May

Vienna, 5th May

Constantinople,(Istanbul)
5th May

Aleppo
7th May

Baghdad, 8th May

Fierce dust storm forces an
emergency desert landing;
waits out storm and continue
on to Baghdad.

Heat and fatigue mak
a difficult landing at a
remote British air bas

Cameron
(Bandar Abbas),
9th May

Karachi
10th May

INDIAN OCEAN

Plane damaged on landing, but repairs are quickly made.

Jhansi, 11th May

Calcutta, 12th May

INDIA

Bay of Bengal

Insein (Rangoon), 13th–15th May

16th Bangkok, May

En route to Singapore, forced off course by heavy rains; stays overnight in Singora.

Singora, 17th May

Singapore 18th May

Equator

ASIA

PACIFIC OCEAN

Tjomal, 19th May

Sourabaya, 20th–21st May

Atamboea, 22nd–23rd May

Darwin, 24th May

Plane's lower wing is pierced by bamboo sticks on landing. Again, repairs slow progress.

Forced landing at nearby Haliluik delays her arrival by a day, causing fears she has crashed.

AUSTRALIA

Mishaps and Adventures

Amy Johnson's solo flight required great courage and determination. Her flight path took her on a perilous journey over oceans, deserts, mountains, and jungles. Much of the route was largely uncharted. The first leg was 1,200 km to Vienna. She then flew to Istanbul, over Turkey's Taurus Mountains to Baghdad, Karachi, Rangoon, Singapore, Java, and Australia. Along the way, she survived storms, a crash landing in Myanmar, and frequent mechanical breakdowns. She had flown 17,700 km – the first woman to fly alone to Australia.

Perilous passage

On the third day, Amy Johnson faced the challenge of Turkey's Taurus Mountains, with peaks as high as 3,600 m. Flying through dense clouds, her wingtips came perilously close to the steep rock faces. Once clear, she continued on to Baghdad.

Record start

Johnson managed to beat Bert Hinkler's time from London to Karachi by two days, but bad weather and the need to make plane repairs delayed her journey in the later stages.

Hope dashed

Approaching Rangoon in rain, Johnson landed safely on a soccer field at Insein, north of Rangoon, only to skid into a ditch. It took three days to repair the damaged fuselage, propeller, and chassis, ending her chances of beating Hinkler's record.

Timor crossing

The final leg was a 800-km passage over the stormy Timor Sea to Darwin. Ditching over open water would spell certain death. On 24th May, a passing oil tanker spotted the *Jason* overhead and radioed Darwin that Amy Johnson was en route.

Celebrity status

Having flown across continents and oceans, Amy Johnson became an instant celebrity. She toured a number of Australian cities.

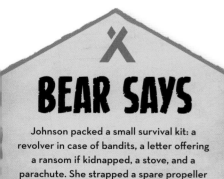

BEAR SAYS

Johnson packed a small survival kit: a revolver in case of bandits, a letter offering a ransom if kidnapped, a stove, and a parachute. She strapped a spare propeller to the fuselage. She recruited local carpenters and mechanics to keep the *Jason* airworthy.

Fame and Fate

Amy Johnson had a brilliant, if brief, career. In 1931, with Jack Humphreys, she made the first one-day flight from London to Moscow. She twice set a world record flying from London to Cape Town, in 1932 and 1936. With her husband, aviator Jim Mollison, she flew in the great MacRobertson Air Race of 1934, a race from England to Australia that remains a major event in the history of world aviation. The pair reached India in record time but struck engine trouble and had to withdraw. During World War II, Johnson ferried warplanes from British factories to operational air bases for the Royal Air Force. On a mission in January 1941, she bailed out into the freezing cold Thames Estuary in rather mysterious circumstances. Her body was never recovered.

Flight gear
Amy Johnson wore the typical flying garb of the 1930s. The leather flight suit and goggles were essential for flying in open-cockpit aircraft.

Amelia Earhart

In 1932, America's Amelia Earhart (left) became the first woman, and the second person after Lindbergh, to fly solo across the Atlantic. She set many records. In 1937, attempting to be the first woman to fly around the world, she and navigator Fred Noonan disappeared without trace over the Pacific Ocean. In 1940, some bones were discovered on an island that have long been believed to be Earhart's, suggesting that she may have survived the crash and died on the island.

Queen of the air

When Johnson departed on 5th May, she was virtually unknown. When she returned in August later the same year she was an international hero. Crowds lined London's streets to welcome Amy Johnson home after her remarkable 19.5-day flight from England to Australia.

BEAR SAYS

Over 85 years since her historic flight, Amy Johnson remains a national icon. Her iconic Gypsy Moth plane, *Jason,* can still be seen at the Science Museum in London.

Voyager

Dick Rutan & Jeana Yeager

The World's Longest Flight

By the mid-1980s, one major record for fixed-wing aircraft had still to be won — no one had even attempted to fly nonstop around the world without refuelling. In December 1986, two American pilots, Dick Rutan and Jeana Yeager, rose to the challenge, flying over four great oceans, across three continents, and through storms to seize victory. It was the world's longest flight to that date, and they almost doubled the world distance record. Luck played little part. They flew their experimental aeroplane, *Voyager,* into the record books with a bold idea, careful planning, expert navigation, and no small amount of courage.

Tight squeeze

Roughly the size of an old-style phone booth, the crew compartment housed the instrument panel, flight controls, a rest area, and storage space for food, drink, and emergency equipment.

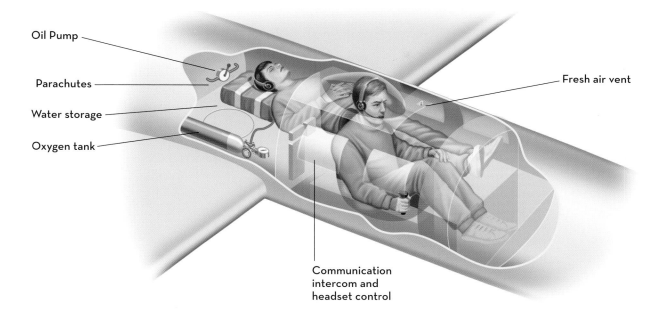

Oil Pump

Parachutes

Water storage

Oxygen tank

Fresh air vent

Communication intercom and headset control

A powered glider

The *Voyager* was a kind of powered glider, with the capacity to stay airborne for days. The wings provided both "flex" and "lift" for the aircraft on its remarkable flight path around the world.

The "flying fuel tank"

The *Voyager* was the brainchild of aircraft designer Burt Rutan and his pilot brother, Dick. Designed specifically to break the world long-distance record, the plane had to be capable of carrying a huge fuel load. It also had to be light, yet strong. The wings and fuselage were made of space-age composite material consisting mainly of graphite, Kevlar, and fibreglass. The aircraft had 17 fuel tanks.

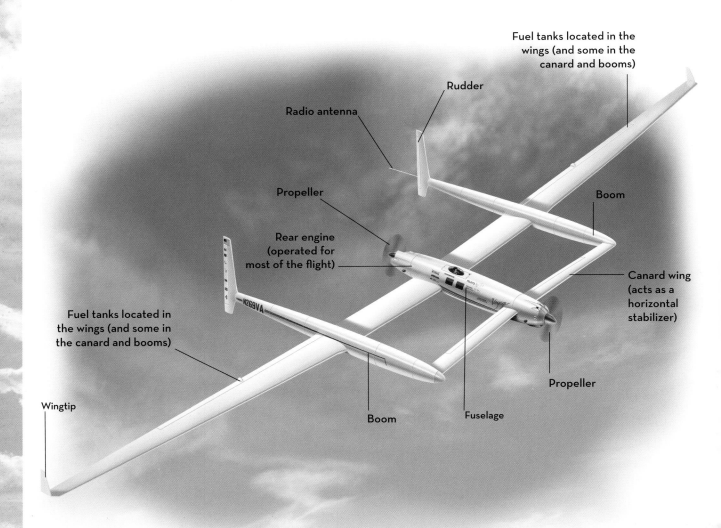

Fuel tanks located in the wings (and some in the canard and booms)

Rudder

Radio antenna

Boom

Propeller

Rear engine (operated for most of the flight)

Canard wing (acts as a horizontal stabilizer)

Fuel tanks located in the wings (and some in the canard and booms)

Propeller

Wingtip

Boom

Fuselage

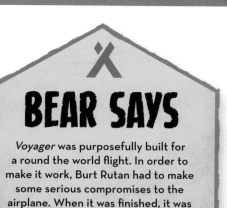

Teledyne Continental engines

The *Voyager* had two Teledyne Continental piston engines, one forward and one aft. The rear engine, a water-cooled ILO-200, operated throughout the flight. The front engine, an air-cooled O-240 type, was used for acceleration and special manoeuvres. Both engines were fuel-efficient and capable of long-duration flights.

Voyager Statistics	
Wingspan including wingtips	33.8 m
Weight of aircraft	1,020.6 kg
Weight of fuel	3,180.4 kg
Number of fuel tanks	17
Gross takeoff weight	4397.4 kg
World flight speed	(official) 186.11 km/h

A smiling Rutan and Yeager stand in front of *Voyager* before their legendary flight.

Nonstop around the Globe

The *Voyager* lifted off the runway at Edwards Air Force Base, California, on the morning of 14th December 1986. On their great adventure, Rutan and Yeager faced many challenges, including bad weather – at one point they had to navigate around Typhoon Marge, a 966-km wide storm in the Pacific – and the need to avoid the air space of hostile countries. They survived several on-board mechanical mishaps. Alone and vulnerable, they depended on their Mission Control team for communications, weather alerts, and technical help. Above all, they had to combat extreme physical and mental fatigue as they fought to keep the unstable *Voyager* on course on such a long and gruelling flight.

Weight watchers

With the heavy fuel load, the weight of supplies and equipment had to be minimized. Food and drink were carefully measured. Maps and navigation aids were essential, along with oxygen for cruising at high altitudes. Survival gear was minimal: two lightweight parachutes, tailored to each pilot, and two small rubber rafts. On the eve of the flight, Jeana Yeager even cut off her long hair.

The long runway

The *Voyager* required almost the entire 4,572 m of the runway at Edwards Air Force Base to take off. Owing to the heavy fuel load, the bouncing wings scraped against the runway and a piece of each wingtip broke off. After circling the field to assess the damage, the pilots decided it was safe to continue the flight.

BEAR SAYS

Adventuring involves a lot of hard work and planning – nearly six years of construction and testing were required before the *Voyager* was ready for its epic journey.

Pioneer pilots

Dick Rutan and Jeana Yeager came from different backgrounds. He had been a fighter pilot in the US Air Force. She was a design drafting engineer and skilled pilot.

Heading toward the coast of Brazil over the open Atlantic Ocean, the *Voyager* flew into a thunderstorm. "We got tossed, like a boat in a big wave", Dick Rutan recalled. At one point, they had to fly the aircraft out of a near-fatal, 90-degree bank.

The Long Haul Begins

The *Voyager* pilots set out to circle the globe at its widest circumference. This meant a nonstop flight of more than 39,000 km. Such a long journey required great discipline and endurance. Each day brought new challenges as they flew through shifting weather fronts or made time-consuming detours to avoid hostile air space. They tried to work in shifts of two to three hours, one flying while the other rested.

Heading west

Voyager followed a westerly flight path to take advantage of the trade winds. The plane was difficult to turn – only the right tail fin had a rudder. The pilot had to be alert at all times. Dick Rutan did most of the flying, but Jeana Yeager took the controls at several critical points.

Venus rising

Off the coast of strife-torn Somalia, flying at night, fear gripped the pilots when what looked like a light from an airplane appeared behind the *Voyager*. Was it a hostile fighter plane? To their great relief, it proved to be the light from Venus, the morning star.

Crisis averted

On the final day, off the coast of Baja, California, the plane's aft engine suddenly shut down. A heart-stopping few moments ensued. Attempts to pump fuel to it failed. The forward engine was hastily ignited, fuel flowed, and the aft engine came to life.

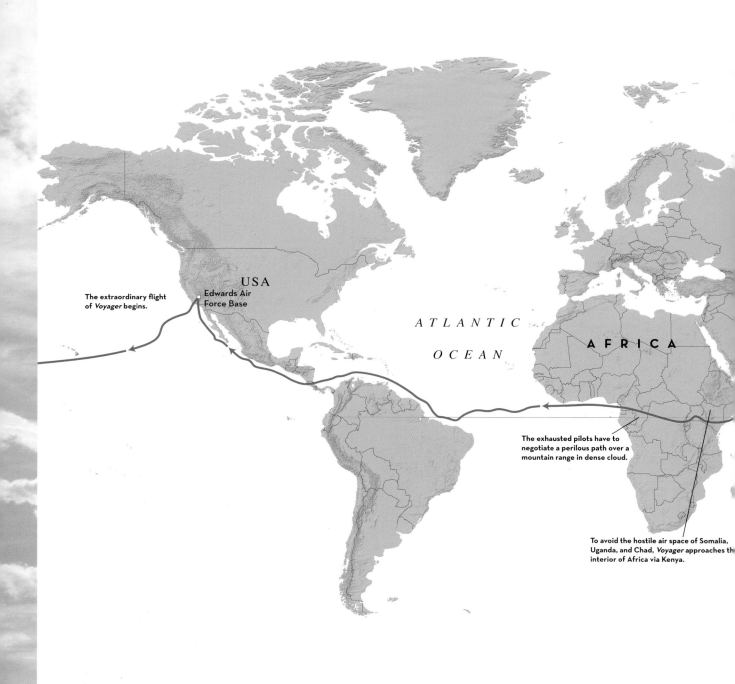

The extraordinary flight of *Voyager* begins.

USA
Edwards Air
Force Base

ATLANTIC

OCEAN

AFRICA

The exhausted pilots have to
negotiate a perilous path over a
mountain range in dense cloud.

To avoid the hostile air space of Somalia,
Uganda, and Chad, *Voyager* approaches th
interior of Africa via Kenya.

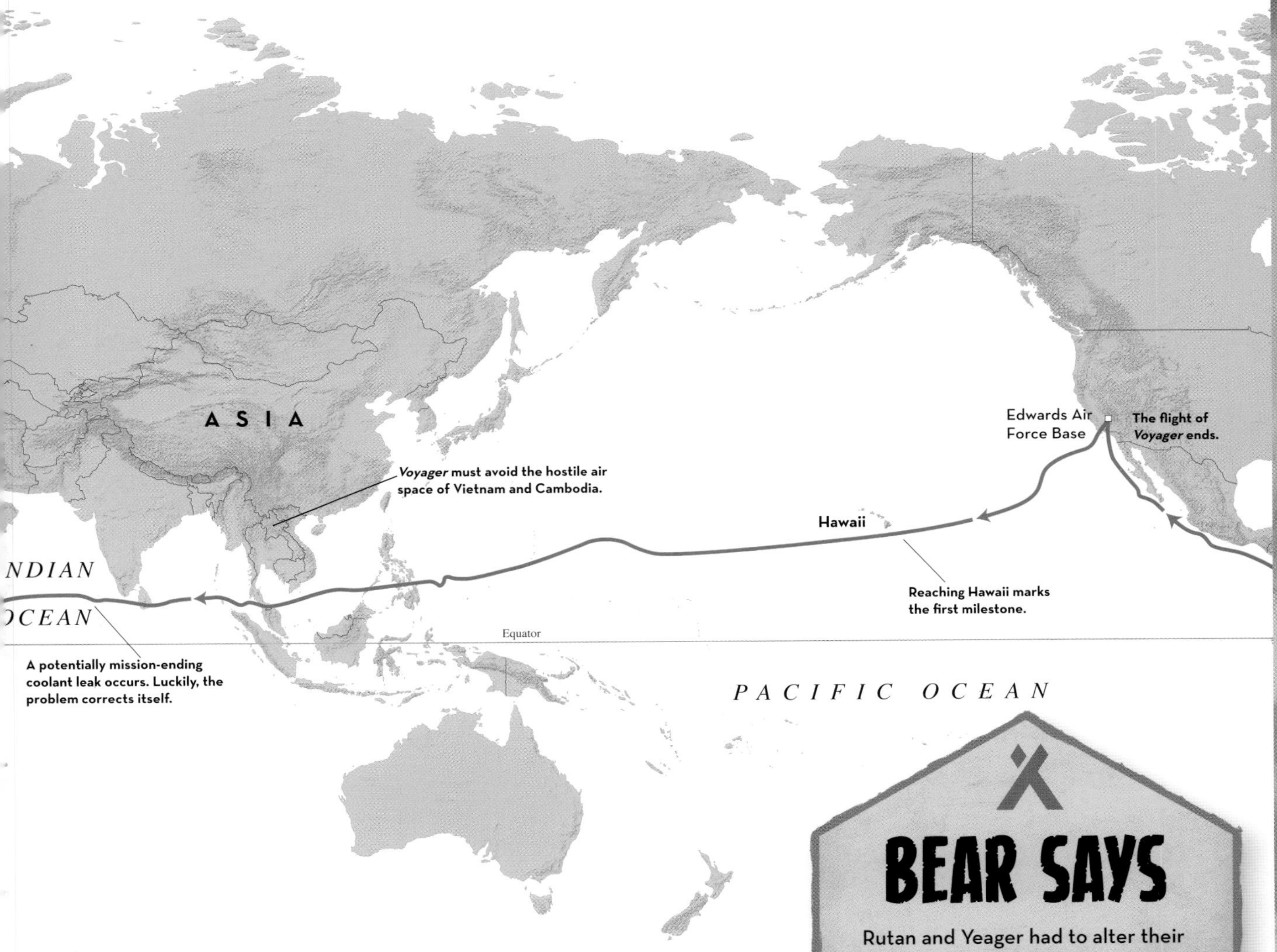

ASIA

Voyager must avoid the hostile air space of Vietnam and Cambodia.

INDIAN OCEAN

A potentially mission-ending coolant leak occurs. Luckily, the problem corrects itself.

Edwards Air Force Base

The flight of *Voyager* ends.

Hawaii

Reaching Hawaii marks the first milestone.

Equator

PACIFIC OCEAN

BEAR SAYS

Rutan and Yeager had to alter their route to avoid bad weather and to stay out of hostile air space, using up precious fuel.

Triumph of the Human Spirit

Nearly exhausted, Dick Rutan landed the *Voyager* at Edwards Air Force Base on 23rd December 1986. Thousands had gathered to welcome the pilots home. The 40,227-km flight had taken 9 days, 3 minutes, and 44 seconds. Even as the *Voyager* landed, an oil seal in the rear engine failed – a reminder of the hazards of such a long flight. Dick Rutan and Jeana Yeager had established a new milestone in aviation. For their remarkable feat, they won aviation's highest honour, the Collier Trophy. The *Voyager* never flew again, but soon found its place at Washington, DC's National Air and Space Museum, with Charles Lindbergh's *Spirit of St. Louis* and other historic aircraft.

The genius of Burt Rutan

Burt Rutan has won huge praise for his aircraft designs. In the 1970s, he experimented with composite materials to design home-built planes. Then came his long-distance aircraft such as the *Voyager* and the *GlobalFlyer*. In 2004, his *SpaceShipOne* became the first privately built spacecraft to reach outer space. With *SpaceShipTwo*, in association with Virgin Galactic, he has paved the way for commercial space flights.

Welcome home

Thousands gathered at Edwards Air Force Base to welcome the *Voyager* home. When the plane landed, after its historic flight lasting just over 216 hours, it had a mere 48 kg of fuel left in the tanks.

National heroes

In recognition of their achievement, President Ronald Reagan awarded the rarely bestowed Presidential Citizen Medal of Honour to Dick and Burt Rutan and Jeana Yeager.

Solo nonstop record

In 2005, Steve Fossett flew Burt Rutan's *GlobalFlyer* on the first solo nonstop flight around the world. Flying at altitudes of 13,716 m, Fossett was in the air for just over 67 hours. The futuristic *GlobalFlyer* consisted of three hulls attached to a 35-m wing. Atop the centre hull was a single jet engine.

Reference

Modern aircraft

Modern aeroplanes have a range of control surfaces, including ailerons, elevators, and a rudder, which redirect the airstream and allow the pilot to maintain direction and altitude in flight. Some basic features of modern planes are shown here.

Spoilers/ airbrakes
These help to reduce altitude without loss of speed. They also enable a plane to slow down rapidly for landing.

Elevators
The elevators are on the tail and control the pitch of the plane.

Flaps
Flaps on the edge of the wing help the aircraft to gain more lift at slower speeds.

Rudder
The rudder controls the yaw of the plane. It is located on the vertical stabilizer on the tail.

Ailerons
The ailerons move in opposite directions from each other and control the aircraft roll.

Slats
Slats on the front of the wing increase lift, especially during take off and landing. They are often retractable.

Controlled flight

An aeroplane can rotate in three different ways, pitch, roll, and yaw. These determine the attitude, or position, of the aircraft while it is in motion through the airstream.

Pitch Movement of the nose of the aircraft upward or downward is called "pitch".

Yaw The pilot controls nose direction left or right, or "yaw", with the rudder.

Roll The wing ailerons control the "roll" or "bank" right or left of the aircraft.

HEADING			
YEAR	**FLIGHT**	**AIRCRAFT/SPACECRAFT**	**PILOT(S)/ASTRONAUT(S)**
1903	First powered and controlled flight	Flyer	Wright brothers
1909	First flight across the English Channel	Blériot XI	Louis Blériot
1912	First woman to fly across the English Channel	Blériot XI	Harriet Quimby
1914	Round-trip from St. Petersburg to Kiev	Il'ya Muromets	Igor Sikorsky
1919	First flight across the North Atlantic	Vickers Vimy bomber	John Alcock and Arthur Brown
1919	First Flight from England to Australia within 30 days	Vickers Vimy bomber	Ross and Keith Smith
1927	First transatlantic flight	Spirit of St. Louis	Charles Lindbergh
1928	First trans-Pacific flight	Fokker trimotor Southern Cross	Charles Kingsford Smith and Charles Ulm
1930	England to Darwin, Australia	DH.60G Gipsy Moth Jason	Amy Johnson
1932	First woman (and second person) to fly solo across the Atlantic	Lockheed Vega 5B	Amelia Earhart
1947	First aircraft to break the sound barrier	Bell X-1 Glamorous Glennis	Charles E. Yeager
1968	First manned spaceflight to leave Earth orbit and orbit the Moon	Apollo 8	Frank Borman, James Lovell, and William Anders
1969	First spaceflight to land people on the Moon	Apollo 11	Neil Armstrong, Michael Collins, and Edwin "Buzz" Aldrin
1986	First nonstop around-the-world plane flight without refuelling	Voyager	Dick Rutan and Jeana Yeager
1999	First nonstop around-the-world balloon flight	Brietling Orbiter 3	Bertrand Piccard and Brian Jones
2004	First privately-owned spacecraft to enter space	SpaceShipOne	Michael Melvill

How spacecraft fly

Beyond Earth's atmosphere, there is no air to produce lift or drag. The main force that spacecraft are subject to is gravity, and thrust is the force that allows a spacecraft to get into space and manoeuvre.

Glossary

Altimeter – A flight instrument used to measure height above Earth.

Altitude – Distance above sea level or land.

Artificial satellite – An object or vehicle designed to orbit Earth, the Moon, or some other celestial body. Used for communications, navigation, and to gather weather data.

Astronaut – A person trained, or in training, to take part in a space flight.

Barnstormer – A pilot who performed stunts in aeroplanes for audiences of air enthusiasts.

Biplane – A fixed-wing aircraft with two pairs of wings, one above the other.

Boom – A structural feature of certain aircraft typically connecting the tail surfaces and the fuselage.

Canard/canard wing – A wing-like structure included on some aircraft that is mounted in front of the main wing(s) and acts as a horizontal stabilizer.

Centrifuge – A rapidly rotating machine used to simulate the rapid acceleration and changes in gravity experienced within a spacecraft.

Cockpit – The compartment containing the controls from where the pilot flies the plane.

Cosmonaut – A Soviet or Russian astronaut.

Eastern daylight time (EDT) – The time along the east coast of North America during daylight saving time.

Fixed-wing aircraft – An aircraft with wings fastened to the fuselage, as distinct from a helicopter.

Fuselage – The main, or core, body of an aircraft.

Mothership – An aircraft designed to carry a smaller aircraft or spacecraft that will be released from it and operate independently of it.

NASA – National Aeronautics and Space Administration: an independent agency of the United States government responsible for aviation and spaceflight.

Orbit – To circle Earth, another planet, or another celestial body.

Quarantine – A set period during which people or animals are kept in isolation to prevent the spread of diseases or pests.

Radar – A device that uses radio beams to navigate and to detect and locate objects in the air.

Rocket – In its simplest form, a device (usually cylinder-shaped) containing liquid or solid fuel which when ignited propels the device forward.

Space probe – A rocket-propelled missile that can travel into space and radio information about its environment back to Earth.

Space walk – Any physical activity performed outside a spacecraft by one of the crew.

Sputnik – The Russian word for artificial satellite. It came into worldwide use after the launch of Sputnik 1 in 1957.

Suborbital – Less than one orbit.

Transponder – A device carried on aircraft that responds to ground-based signals to provide air traffic controllers with information about the aircraft's altitude and position.

Index

Picture credits

1 06photo; 3 Gamma-Rapho; 4t Bettmann, c Ruben Sprich, b isoft; 5t NASA, c Bettmann, b Bettmann; 6 NBC; 7t Dan Kitwood, b Handout; 8 Bettmann; 9 Bettmann; 10t Keystone-France, b Roger Viollet; 11 Bettmann, b Hulton Archive; 12r Kamira; 13l Time Life Pictures; 14r Santi Visalli, c Bettmann, b Universal History Archive; 15t Bettmann, b Jane McIlroy; 16 Christophel Fine Art; 17t George Silk, c Hulton Archive, b Bettmann; 17 Keystone-France; 19 Bettmann; 20 Hulton Archive; 21t Bettmann, c Ulrich Baumgarten, Bettmann; 24cr Roger Viollet, c Universal Images Group, b Time Life Pictures; 25tr Bettmann, c spatuletail, b Tony Evans; 26 Gamma-Rapho; 27t Gamma-Rapho, b Hulton Archive; 28 Gamma-Rapho; 29 Gamma Rapho; 30 Gamma Rapho; 31t iamnong, b Gamma-Rapho; 34b Gamma-Rapho; 35t NASA; 36 Gamma-Rapho; 38 Universal History Archive; 40 Ruben Sprich; 41 Gamma Rapho; 42 Vixit; 43t Bear Grylls Ventures, b Ullstein Bild; 44t Crystal Image, bl AFT, br ueuaphoto; 45l The Sydney Morning Herald, r Corbis Sport; 46 ktsdesign; 47t Bear Grylls Ventures, b M.Khebra; 48t Rene Holtslag, b R.M. Nunes; 49t Peter Hermes FUrian, b AFP; 50 ubon shinghasin; 51 Punnawit Suwattanun; 52 Jason Maehl; 53 Bear Grylls Ventures; 54 Jacques Loic; 55 Olga Danulenko; 56 Vixittill; 27 Globe Turner, LLC; 58 Bear Grylls Ventures; 58-59 isoft; 60 Anton ROgozin; 61 Bear Grylls Ventures; 62 NASA; 63t NASA/Getty, c Universal History Archive, b Juergen Faelchle; 64tl NASA, tr NASA, bl Sovfoto, br NASA; 65-70 NASA; 72 NASA; 80 NASA, 81cl NASA, cr NASA, b Handout; 82 Bettmann; 83t Museum of Flight Foundation, b Time Life Pictures; 84 Time Life Pictures; 85l DeAgostini, r Ullstein Bild; 88 Bettmann; 89t Sean Pavone, b gaborbasch; 90 Hulton Archive; 91l Everett Historical, r Hulton Archive; 92 Paul Harris; 93b Bettmann; 95096 Bettmann; 97 Paul Harris; 98 KHH 1971; 99t Dennis van de Water, b Andrea Izzotti; 102 Paul Harris; 103t Bettmann, c The Life Images Collection, b WireImage; 105 NASA

All other images © Weldon Owen, an Imprint of King's Road Publishing